T5-BBB-503

INFORMATION RESOURCES AND CORPORATE GROWTH

EDITED BY EDUARDO PUNSET
AND GERRY SWEENEY

First published in Great Britain in 1989 by
Pinter Publishers Limited
25 Floral Street, London WC2E 9DS

British Library Cataloguing in Publication Data

A CIP catalogue record for this book is available from the British Library

ISBN 0 86187 720 9

Library of Congress Cataloging-in-Publication Data

Information resources and corporate growth/edited by Eduardo Punset and Gerry Sweeney.
187 + v pp., 21.0 x 14.8cm.
Includes index.
ISBN 0-86187-720-9
1. Information resources management. I. Punset, Eduard, 1936-
II. Sweeney, G. P. (Gerald Patrick), 1928-
T58.64.153 1988
658.4'038--dc19 88-39499
CIP

Typeset by Dublin Online Typographic Services, Dublin, Ireland
Printed and bound in Great Britain by Biddles Ltd, Guildford and King's Lynn

Contents

Foreword

The economies of the 21st Century are breaking out of the straitjacket of conventional economic policy. Until very recently, people were led to believe that, in practice, economic policy turned around the consolidated balance sheet of the banking sector. Since net domestic assets equalled currency in circulation (on the liabilities side of the balance sheet) less net international assets, by the sheer logic of double entry accounting, one only needed to push down domestic credit to improve the external balance. This assumed of course some sort of correlation between expected GNP growth and money supply.

Only gradually does everyone seem to realise that whilst induced changes in the accounts may have contributed positively to a sounder financial system they do not induce growth. They have left virtually untouched the propensity of people to innovate, to push for technical change through old fashioned optimisation schemes and to improve the level of technical culture. Since job creation only thrives where a given level of technical culture is reached allowing people to risk and to innovate, it is no wonder that an increasing number of economists are taking a closer look at innovation policies in the face of persistent unemployment.

A preliminary and overriding conclusion is now showing up; with identical quality levels of physical inputs some firms are unable to succeed while others fare very well. The competitive edge seems to lie in the management of intangible assets such as information flows from suppliers and customers, know-how and technology, access to knowledge intensive networks, corporate alliances rather than mergers, brand care and corporate culture.

Hence the need to congratulate the Instituto de Empresa for convening in Madrid the *European Conference on Information: The Key Asset* for corporate and regional growth, of which selected papers are published here. The work was made possible by the generous support of the Commission of the European Communities under its SPRINT programme and of the Madrid Regional Government.

Eduardo Punset
Instituto de Empresa

1. Introduction: information and corporate growth

Gerry Sweeney

SICA Innovation Consultants
Dublin

Never before in the history of mankind have so many people and such a large proportion of the labour force been employed in activities related to the generation, acquisition, processing, communication and diffusion of information (see Lamberton, Ch. 2 in this volume). Yet there are widely divergent views as to what is and what is not information or an information activity. It is a complex concept, embracing ideas and knowledge, the contents of libraries, office files and computers and even more that combination of education, experience, skills, intuition and creativity which is both the substance and the output of the human mind. Under the term 'technical progress', the continuing changes in scientific, technical and managerial knowledge and know-how, it is the residual and intangible factor which has been responsible for the major proportion of economic growth (Dennison 1974). As an intangible it is difficult to measure.

It is equally difficult to measure and to price as a corporate asset, and it therefore rarely appears on the agenda of a management or board meeting or on the curriculum of a management school or conference. It does not fit easily into the numerically based management philosophies or finance-oriented management structures which are dominant in much of Europe and North America. Yet the empirical evidence strongly indicates that it is the quality of the information activities and of the information possessed by a firm which make its innovations commercially successful and give it competitive edge. In information, its acquisition and exploitation, lies the key to the creation of economic wealth and corporate growth.

The chapters in this book explore various aspects of information, its management, its role and its local roots. The specific steps to be taken in formulation of a corporate information strategy are not set out. That is the function of each firm. The concepts and principles which should permeate the formulation of strategy and the attitudes of management are, however, given including aspects of the relationship between a firm's prosperity and that of its local or regional environment.

From the beginning

The role of information begins before the birth of a company. Successful entrepreneurship is based on superior information. New companies are founded by entrepreneurs on the basis of some perception of an innovative opportunity. They possess already a diversity of information in their education, training and experience, and diversity is correlated with conception of an innovative idea and with entrepreneurial vitality (Sweeney 1987). The new firm is founded around the skills and experience of the founder or founding team. These skills are the initial technological core, but the opportunity is perceived through a matching of these skills with information on user needs or market openings. Before start-up the successful entrepreneur minimises risk by increasing his store of information. He indulges in an intensive process of information gathering from consultants, business friends, sources of finance, market gurus, people in the know or people who know people in the know. The quality of his information sources and channels is critical to success.

This superior information is a product of the characteristics of the entrepreneur. The successful entrepeneur would seem to be more active in the search for information, sharper in identifying information of relevance and more efficient in processing information. How can corporations emulate these capabilities of the founding entrepreneur? That there is a problem can be perceived from a headline in *the Financial Times* (1988). 'Japan may make biggest gains from single market'. It reported a study by the Henley Centre, a British economic consulting firm. The gains will not come from take-overs of European firms, but by direct gaining of competitive advantage.

Unlike much of European and North American management, Japanese management tends to seek corporate growth not through take-over but through an organic growth based on management of information. They have a clearer appreciation of information and concentrate management effort on its acquisition, diffusion and control. Even when faced with decline in existing business such as in textiles, the response of Japanese management in investing in new business areas has been to invest in R & D and related information generating activities. They have bought themselves out of difficulties not by acquiring existing firms but by acquiring information. No doubt not all Japanese firms behave like this, but equally it is a style of management long known in Europe. The surprise is that it is not more widely practised.

Characteristics of progressive firms

Some thirty years ago, Charles Carter and Bruce Williams (1957) published a pioneering study which has become the reference point for research on innovative and progressive firms. They had surveyed some 500 British firms to discover the characteristics which distinguished technically progressive firms from the rest. A technically progressive firm was defined as one which on a necessarily subjective judgement is keeping within a reasonable distance of the best current practice and is commercially successful.

Of the 500 studied only fifty were considered to be progressive. There were some twenty-five specific characteristics identified as distinguishing the progressive from the non-progressive and most were concerned with some aspect of information and communication. Briefly, they were:

High quality of incoming information.
Readiness to look outside the firm.
Willingness to share knowledge. i.e. own information and knowledge with outsiders.
Willingness to take new knowledge on licence and to enter joint ventures.
Effective internal communication and co-ordination.
Deliberate survey of incoming information and potential ideas.
Consciousness of costs and profits in the research and development departments (if there were R & D departments).
Identifying the outcome of investment decisions.
Use of management techniques i.e. effective use of best practices.
High status of scientists and technologists in the firm.
Use of scientists and technologists on the board.
High quality in the chief executive(s).
Ability to attract talented people.
Sound policy of recruitment for management.
Willingness to arrange for effective training of staff.
Adequate provision for intermediate managers.
An ability to bring the best out of managers.
Effective selling policy.
Good technical service to customers.
Ingenuity in getting around material and equipment shortages.
Readiness to look ahead.
High rate of expansion.

Rapid replacement of machines, high proportion of new equipment.
Larger development teams.

It is a long list of specific items, but that does not account for the real lack of take-up by British and North American management in particular. Rothwell (Gardiner and Rothwell 1985) in a booklet to mark the opening of an Innovation Centre by the British Design Council, remarks that 'Unfortunately the lessons learned from the pioneering research were not generally taken up by the British industry'. Leading into a summary of the findings of the series of studies carried out under Project SAPPHO, Rothwell continues, 'Once again the take-up of the results of these studies was only slight. Perhaps the main reason for this ... is that none of the studies yielded prescriptions or recipes for success, but rather they offered simply a set of broad guidelines and identified crucial areas for management action'.

Possibly the most revealing evidence of the lack of take-up were the 'discoveries' of Peters and Waterman (1982) of the characteristics of firms in search of excellence. They demonstrated again the phenomenon of the time lag of thirty to sixty years between generation of knowledge by research and its application and that management consultants are not an exception in their rate of take-up.

Project SAPPHO examined sets of pairs of closely related innovations, one a commercial failure, the other a success (Rothwell 1977). The characteristics which distinguished the successful from the unsuccessful can be summarised as:

1. Quality of management style: open and horizontal management style; high-quality managers.
2. Marketing and user needs: meeting of identified user need or market opportunity with a vigorous marketing and sales policy.
3. After-sales service and user education: efficient customer-support services.
4. Good communication and effective collaboration.
5. Efficient internal and external communication, such as direct personal links to scientific and technical expertise specifically relevant to the product being developed, and close collaboration with users during the development process.
6. Efficient development work: bugs eliminated before the innovative product enters the market.
7. Key individuals: a person of authority who takes a direct interest in the innovation and supports its progress.
8. Innovation as a corporate-wide task: harmonious co-operation and co-ordination between the various functions involved in the innovation process.

A learning system

The emphasis is again on information and external and internal communication and on learning from technological and market sources. The last finding is particularly interesting since Carter and Williams found that having a formally constituted R & D department was not a characteristic of progressive firms. They might have one or they might not. What they have is a constant search for improvement in each functional area, a search for and adoption of the best practice in their own particular operations and a sharing of expertise in the development of new products as in the last of the SAPPHO findings. In Chapter 7 of this book Sciberras refers to informal effort to achieve technical change in a balanced fashion across key functional areas as often being not only more critical to competitive success but also as costing more than the formal R & D effort. Formal R & D is a focused effort, but too often in Taylorist hierarchies an isolated one, to obtain and evaluate information. The informal gains its effectiveness rating because each area is in search of excellence within a structure with low departmental barriers.

Shackle, one of the pioneers of the economics of information and knowledge, stated that 'the business of living and within that larger whole the business of producing and exchanging goods, essentially and inescapably involves and requires the continuous and endless gaining of knowledge. To say that there is always potential new knowledge to be gained is to say that possessed knowledge is always incomplete, unsure and potentially wrong' (Shackle 1970). Decision is the abandonment of an old policy and the adoption of a new one; it is the invention of new policies, even policies that were beyond the mind's reach, that were logically non-existent, with the knowledge formerly possessed. In a business, profit is the instigator of radical rethinking and reform of policy. Positive or negative, it measures the extent to which expectation of the future has proved fallible, the degree to which the information on which that expectation was based has proved accurate. Success is the outcome of the quality of the information processes and their management. Inevitably, one is drawn to the concept that the pursuit of profit is the pursuit of knowledge (Sweeney 1975).

Against the kind of empirical results produced by Carter and Williams and by Rothwell and reinforced in specific aspects by many other researchers, one is lead further to the conclusion that the progressive firm is a learning system, possessing a stock of knowledge and continuously enaged in reaching out to acquire new information and knowledge with which to adjust and add to its stock. It is structured to pursue information not profit. Profit is the measure of its success in the pursuit of information and knowledge. Jacob Marschak's statement (1968) that the major activities of a modern economy are enquiring, communicating (including evaluating) and deciding is a succinct description of this microeconomic unit, the progressive firm, and it reflects the views put forward by Hiro Itami (Ch. 4 below) from his observations of Japanese firms.

Itami's view is that information and knowledge under their various guises such as technological, marketing and managerial skills or brand name and reputation are the key invisible assets, in the sense that they are the assets which give a firm its competitive edge. His view is a further corroboration that the progressive firm is one structured to pursue information.

A firm has a stock of knowledge and exists in the framework of three information flows - from the environment into the firm, internally within the firm and from the firm to the environment of customers, suppliers and so on. It is the function of management to control these flows and that Japanese manufacturing firms have excelled in this is measured by their 'high rate of expansion', which Carter and Williams described as the rate of increase of assets, through organic growth.

In contrast there are the firms which focus on the visible financial asset and take a short-term view of investment pay-back and profit. They lose in long-term growth and in creation of new economic wealth.

Core competence and competitive edge

One can look on the firm and its stock of knowledge as a portfolio of core competences (see Doz, Ch. 5 in this volume). Conventional strategy has put the emphasis on individual product lines and product markets and has looked at the individual business units of the firm. Instead the firm should be considered as a portfolio of competences, technological, marketing and so on. Strategy is the nurturing of these competences and their exploitation in multiple markets and business opportunities. Company success and therefore competitive advantage begins with the differentiation and quality of these competences. In other words, the differentiation and competences on which competitive edge is gained and new wealth created are due to differences in management of the information flows, their use to build the stock of knowledge and their application of this stock to new business opportunities. The difference between those with competitive edge and those without is the difference in informational efficiency which Lamberton (in Ch. 2 below) identifies as distinguishing between regions which generate their own prosperity and those which do not.

Doz puts forward this viewpoint against the background of the difficulties of European corporations in global competition. For the most part these are decentralised, diversified multi-divisional organisations, and they are essentially conglomerates managed as investment portfolios. Whilst large overall, they are relatively small in a particular technology, product or business area. They are therefore weak competitors in global markets. Their decentralised divisions compete with one another for share of the physical assets and each stands alone in its particular market. They do not nurture and share their technical competences to accrue a competitive edge or to optimise a business opportunity. The information flows internally are weak. The kind of decentralisation followed has not been within a strong common culture. It has weakened rather than strengthened the firms, a point stressed in a report on the British electronics industry prepared for the National Economic Development Council (McKinsey 1988).

Impact of information technology

Entering relatively recently into this world in which organisation to pursue information and the management of information flows form the route to competitive edge is information technology. It is a technology pervasive of all aspects of business and of all sectors of manufacturing. It is the major force in the shift from the industrial era to an era in which it will be the dominant technology. Together with globalisation of competition and markets, it is driving the firm to new forms of organisation (see Lamborghini, Ch. 6 in this volume). All firms are adopting the technology with positive or negative effect, but it is to firms which are both producers and intensive users of the technology, such as Olivetti, that one must turn to perceive the present and future impact on strategy and organisation.

We are in an in-between state, a state of discontinuity between the industrial age and the information technology age. To understand the nature of the changes, one must begin with the future organisation and roles of the factory and the office, which are now converging. The technology is moving the factory, the traditional centre of gravity of the firm, further along a road of automation which began with the Industrial Revolution. The factory of the future, however, will be a totally new concept. The factory is under increasing external pressures from the market for flexibility, quality and diversity or customisation. Flexible manufacturing systems are but a step towards meeting these requirements. The factory of the future will be a computer-integrated manufacturing environment which will be integrated with the other strategic areas of the firm. Its output will be not only the material products but also the immaterial information flows, which have traditionally been the prerogative of the office. It will have the capacity to interact in a creative way with the company and with the external environment.

The office under the pressure of the technology and of the need to manage the invisible assets will gradually assume the role of being the centre of gravity of the firm, the centre of its networking. In other words, it will be organised to pursue information.

The technology will thus not only reinforce the more horizontal structure by enhancing communication flows but make of the firm a network of independent companies in a global sense and a network of business units, profit centres, within each company. Globalisation is made possible by the technology but is also itself a driving force, opening frontiers, protected niches and oligopolistic environments. The technology and internal and external pressures push towards decentralised organisation, but to be competitive a strong central strategy based on the core competence of the firm is necessary. The essence of the strategy is the corporate culture, which Itami defines as the distinctive characteristics of the patterns of information processing shared by the members of an organisation. The independent units are integrated by the strategy and the technology, and thus there is a continuing reinforcement of the stock of knowledge through the information flows.

Bureaucracy and flexibility

Opportunities for exploitation of the core competences in new areas of business can be seized because corporate strategy and culture control and permeate each company and unit. Autonomy ensures that the decision-making not only enhances the operational efficiency and effectiveness of the company or unit but also the flexibility and responsiveness to meet customer needs and to seize new opportunities. In today's market, purchasing decisions are being increasingly based on the non-price factors such as diversity, customisation, quality and service. These conditions put a premium on flexibility and speed of response. The rigid hierarchical and bureaucratic structures of the Taylorist or Fordist era with their vertical information flows and rigid centralised information processing and decision-making are no longer appropriate.

As Newton (Ch. 11 below) - who researched computer-based innovations in Canada - concluded, technological change, organisational redesign and human resource policies must go hand in hand: 'You can't put twenty-first-century technology into a nineteenth century workplace'. Concepts and structures appropriate to the industrial era are barriers to progress in the information or information technology era.

The hierarchical bureaucracy has been the organisational phenomenon of the scientific management phase of the industrial era. It is essentially an information-processing organisation, set up to control the complex processes and information inputs required for large-scale production and distribution of standardised products which competed on the basis of price.

The skill and other information inputs removed from the production system as scientific management was applied were taken up by the bureaucracy. Scientific management principles were applied to the organisation of the bureaucracy through compartmentalisation and specialisation. Only those at the centre could see the entire process. Bureaucracies grew larger with increasing numbers of layers. There was a self-reinforcing effect. Large bureaucracies in one sector stimulated their growth in another. Corporate and government bureaucracies become mutually reinforcing in structures and functional locations. The domination of the large bureaucracies in modern economies led to the conclusion that 'an information economy is largely bureaucratic in nature; decisions are made and power is wielded not by many independent firms competing for a market but by relatively insulated private and public bureaucracies' (Porat 1978).

This is changing at least at the more innovative edges of markets and within those firms growing organically. Elsewhere the era of mega take-overs seems to indicate yet further growth in bureaucracies and may itself be the defensive reaction of already large bureaucracies finding difficulty in competing on the basis of their invisible technological, marketing and related information assets. They are Fordist institutions in crisis (see Hepworth, Ch. 3 in this volume). The progressive firms which create new markets through innovation and technical competence and therefore the new economic growth are a minority.

Information is human capital and the information society into which all industrialised countries are entering is the era of human capital in which the information component of the end-product will determine competitiveness. The market is demanding this information component in the technological excellence, design, close matching of customer needs, performance in use, consistency and reliability of its purchases. To meet these demands requires flexible production systems in which groups of workers can see the total process and apply their skills directly to identifying and solving problems. Necessarily, information must flow fully and easily between the groups in the different functional areas of the organisation. Initiative and responsibility must characterise each group to respond to change and opportunity in the environment. In the markets of the future a firm cannot afford the rigid hierarchical chains of command.

Information is people

Nor can it afford the rigid divisions and the narrow telescopic view inherent in the Taylorist system. The wider peripheral vision necessary to see the total process and the sharing in the corporate culture to understand the company in its global context of customers and competitors requires a different approach from the Taylorist to human resource and skill development. As Itami says, each business operation has an output in terms of the invisible assets, and often this output is embodied in the knowledge, skills and judgement of the employee. He quotes an entrepreneur: 'Matsuhita is a company that creates people'. Human skills and capabilities are as much an output of a business operation as the physical products. A company must ensure this output because it is in the business of developing its competence by adding to the skills and widening the experience of its people.

One aspect of this broadening of experience is the Japanese practice of horizontal transfer of junior and middle managers through different functions and locations. They thus acquire a wide understanding of the company and its environment. The practice also develops the communication linkages and lowers barriers between functions and departments. Another aspect is the statement of a Toyota executive that 'when recruiting, what we look for is someone who understands cars and what the customer wants in a car; we will teach him to be a welder'.

The dependence on people, their skills and the polyvalency of their skills is increasing at a time when it seemed to many that technology was taking over. In fact the contribution of human know-how has never been more critical (see Mathis, Ch. 12 below). The information technologies involve end-users' intellectual capabilities. The trend in the shift from low-skilled to skilled professionals is reinforced by the technology (see Newton, Ch. 10 below) and leads to a demand for further training. The market pressures for information-intensive products reinforce the need for people-embodied skills. As Zegveld notes (in Ch. 11 of this volume) large corporations are increasingly creating their own education and training systems, even to doctorate level.

Borum investigated skills and training in software development and programming and found that the same requirement for polyvalency exists (see Ch. 9 below). People working in this area tend to be specialists in a functional or application area who have acquired IT skills or vice versa. IT specialists are now also to be found in the functional application areas. The pervasiveness of IT is fudging the boundaries, and perhaps more than that. In Germany the introduction of computerisation in machine tools initiated a trend to push the organisation into a more Taylorist mode with loss of responsibility by machinists. This gradually reversed under the pressures of quality. The tendency is now one of enhancing the machinists' skills by training in programming. He has thereby control of the total process.

As information technology is intensively applied and assimilated into a company's business operations, it assumes the shape of the company's internal and external information flows. It becomes a means of further enhancing these to gain competitive advantage or to create totally new business (see Griffiths, Ch. 8 below). For example, customers are an invisible asset of the firm. As Itami sees them, they store information about the firm, its reputation and brand name. These are identified in the customers' mind, personal and corporate, with the technology, quality and service, the competitive edge, of the company.

Information technology provides a way of locking the customer in yet further by making him directly part of the technological network of the company and by providing him with information and an immediate direct communication which gives him a competitive advantage in service to his customer. The TOPS videotex service of the Thompson travel group to travel agents is one example.

Or as Griffiths indicated, it may be the information accummulated over many years by the firm which is the source of new business. It is the technology, however, which enables the information to be exploited. The information accumulated about the buying habits of customers through the mail-order business can be processed by Sears to enhance this business and to sell as a value-added product to other businesses. The technology has made this processing possible. The Reuters international news network became a fast-growth financial information service business because the new business opportunities of the information technologies were perceived and exploited.

Competitive edge and local roots

The strategy of a firm operating in large and global markets has become a complex interaction of information technology, human resources and corporate competence. But no firm stands alone. At the global level, Doz and Lamborghini point to the networks of partnerships between large corporations, extending technological competences, creating new business opportunities, bringing new networks of customers within reach and stretching across continents. Yet inside this framework of globalisation lies the need, identified by Lamborghini, for local roots, for each company of the corporation to be embedded in the locality in which it is placed and lives. The justification for such an attitude lies in the information processes which govern innovation and the creation of new economic activities.

Self-generated and self-sustained economic development is a local phenomenon. One has only to look at the maps of any country to recognise that some places generate their own wealth and others do not, some once did but are now in decline. North-Rhine Westphalia once led German prosperity; Munich and Stuttgart now are more significant in terms of new economic wealth. The process of creation of economic wealth begins with the entrepreneur who founds a new firm to manufacture an innovative product or provide a wealth-creating service.

He founds this firm in the locality where he finds the inspiration and the opportunity. The richness, openness and diversity of the information flows stimulate creativity, innovative ideas, and within the locality it is possible to carry out that intensive information-gathering and resource-generating whcih enables the idea to become a market reality.

As the firm grows, the networks of local suppliers of visible and invisible assets and of inputs to the production process become more extensive and intensive. The technological core of entrepreneurial skills initially had its origin in the university/educational research system or apprenticeship system of the locality and was extended and diversified by the incubating firm where he worked previously. As the young firm grows, the network of inputs becomes more complex. Whilst it grows organically as a technically progressive firm, it relies for much of its innovation and flexibility on local smaller suppliers. The system becomes cumulatively self-reinforcing. More firms grow large and more new small firms are founded, more information-intensive and specialist services locate nearby.

The locality develops an autonomy of information: within half an hour it is possible to have an information intensive face-to-face contact. The locality has superior information. In Chapter 3 Hepworth refers to 47 per cent of occupations in the south-east of England as being information occupations as against 38 per cent in the north-east. Some 45 per cent of public- and private-sector research is located in the south-east and so on. Molle (Ch. 14 below) highlights the concentration of R & D in the European Community. Paris and Madrid show a similar pattern, but one which, like the English south-east, was also heavily influenced by the strong centralisation of government, itself a provider of information and resources. The private and public information-intensive functions and occupations form the quaternary or information sector (see Lamberton, Ch. 2 below), which is the source of a prosperous locality's superior information.

This sector is a determining influence on the ability of an entrepreneur to found a company and on the ability of the company to grow into a large corporation and to be competitive as a large corporation. It determines that A in this region knows more than B in that and has faster access. Regions like companies can be distinguished by their informational efficiency, their ability to manage their invisible assets. Their informational efficiency determines the rate of foundation of new firms, their survival and the ability of some to grow large. It is no accident that many Japanese and US multinationals remain deeply routed in their birthplace.

Where informational efficiency does not exist within a region, then it fails to generate its own growth (see Casey, Ch. 13 below). This raises questions as to the degree and mode of government intervention to stimulate growth or to prevent decline. The information flows which in practice stimulate innovation and create the competitive edge by continuous enrichment of the stock of knowledge and the competences of a firm are largely informal. In Chapter 11 Zegveld discusses how an intensive network of industrial extension officers modelled on the US Agricultural Extension Service, such as is being set up in the Netherlands, could stimulate the networks between the university and research infrastructure and small and new firms and thus develop a higher informational efficiency. It is a model in operation in other countries, but nowhere so intensively as in the Netherlands.

In Chapter 12 Mathis describes a programme in which information technology is being applied with the objective of so improving the efficiency of the information flows that the textile industry of Prato will maintain its global leadership. Prato is an area where the former flannel industry and its large producers collapsed and economic prosperity has been restored and increased by an entrepreneurial dynamism in which local banks, chambers of commerce and other organisations have taken part as members of one large industrial organisation. Can such an intervention by a state agency play its role in maintaining the competitiveness of the regional industrial organisation? The Basque problem is different (see Llorens, Ch. 15 below). Here is a region in crisis but with a strong tradition in engineering. The approach has been for the Basque Autonomous Government with the two regional governments to set up infrastructure and subsidy programmes to promote the adoption and diffusion of information technology on a wide scale. The interplay between a firm and its region and their interdependence can be so intimate that progressive regions exhibit characteristics analogous to those of progressive firms described by

Carter and Williams (Sweeney 1987) and they assume structures as industrial organisations themselves. The models of industrial organisation which have evolved in different regions show marked differences. The Stuttgart model has very large firms working in close harmony with smaller suppliers who supply to other customers and other markets and who, because of their informationally rich relationship with their large customers, are internationally competitive. There is the Turin-Fiat model in which Fiat has very many small suppliers who, whilst independent, are also captive to Fiat. There is also the Prato model, which is matched in other regions of Italy. In this model there are very large numbers of very small firms in a sector each specialising in a narrow segment of the total process, with equally small firms scouring the world for orders and information and co-ordinating production to meet the orders. The informal informational networks are intense, but an efficiency in diversified and flexible production of higher-quality goods with economies of scale is achieved at a level impossible in a large corporation.

Nevertheless, Prato being at one extreme of regional industrial organisation with Turin at the other demonstrates that one cannot view the technically progressive industrial corporation as a stand-alone entity. Where a firm maintains the characteristics of a technically progressive firm as a learning system, the evidence seems to indicate that it maintains its roots in the locality where it first flourished - it remains part of the regional industrial organisation. Its technological competence and its culture are inextricably linked into those of the locality. Where a firm abandons its origins and moves headquarters and other information intensive activities to another locality, this seems to be because it has switched the focus of its strategy from its invisible assets to its visible financial assets.

Maintenance of its own technical competence and competitive edge means that the firm is also involved in the maintenance of the competence, the superior information, of the region or locality in which it has its roots. This maintenance is a mutually reinforcing process of two-way information flows between the members of the regional industrial organisation, each nourishing the competence of the other.

Conclusion

The lack of take-up of Carter and Williams and SAPPHO reflects the relatively small minority of larger firms which are progressive and innovative. Doz implies that most large European corporations are not. Itami refers to the small but increasing number of managers who perceive that the key assets are the information-based invisible ones. The evidence as to the optimum route to organic growth and global competitiveness is clear but it is a human characteristic to take the easier route even though it is known not to be the best.

Expenditure on information is capital. So too is the creation of the information channels and the organisational capability to enquire, communicate and decide. Management focus on the invisible assets might be sharpened if an improved accounting system could be devised to reflect the value of the assets which differentiate one company from another in the market (see Lamberton, Ch. 2 below).

References

Carter, C. F., and Williams, B. R. (1957) *Industry and Technical Progress*. Oxford: Oxford University Press.

Dennison, E. F. (1974) *Why Growth Rates Differ: Post-war Experience in Nine Different Countries*. Washington, DC: The Brookings Institution.

Financial Times (1988) 'Japan may make biggest gains from single market'. 27 June.

Gardiner, P., and Rothwell, R. (1985) *Innovation: A Study of the Problems and Benefits of Product Innovation*. London: Design Council.

McKinsey & Co. (1988) 'Electronic industry faces harsh home truths'. *Financial Times*, 27 June.

Marschak, J., (1968) 'Economies of enquiring, communicating, deciding'. *American Economic Review* 58: 1-18.

Peters, T. J. and Waterman, R. H. (1982) *In Search of Excellence*. New York: Harper & Row.

Porat, M. V. (1978) 'Communication policy in an information society, in G. O. Robinson, (ed.) *Communications for Tomorrow*, New York: Praeger.

Rothwell, R. (1977) 'The characteristics of successful innovators and technically progressive firms'. *R & D Management* 7(3): 191-206.

Shackle, G. L. S. (1970) *Expectation, Enterprise and Profit*. London: Allen & Unwin.

Sweeney G. P. (1975) 'The pursuit of knowledge'. *The Information Scientist* 9(2): 51-65.

(1976) *Innovation Entrepreneurs and Regional Development*. London: Frances Pinter.

(1987) 'The entrepreneurial firm as a learning system in the information economy' *The Information Society*, 5: 91-9.

2. The regional information economy: its measurement and significance

D. McL. Lamberton
Information Research Unit
Department of Economics
University of Queensland

The collection of papers in this volume rightly emphasises the efficient exploitation of information resources as a source of competitive advantage. It rightly emphasises information rather than information technology. There has been massive investment in hardware, but in the words of the most recent Nobel winner in economics, 'You can see the computer age everywhere but in the productivity statistics' (Solow). It also emphasises regions and so paves the way for a comparative approach on the part of the social scientist.

The earliest contribution on regional economics in my personal library is a paper by William Weld, 'Regional comparison and economic progress', in Tugwell's *The Trend of Economics* (1924). Weld believed comparative regional economics both lent itself to inductive principles and could contribute to economic well-being. He observed the inequalities of standards of living in different regions and advocated a 'thorough-going search for the causes of the differences'. He recognised many, interacting causes and sought quantification. He added '[their] very differences may be illuminating'. In that spirit, I wish to highlight one particular difference: the extent of exploitation of information resources.

The basic question we are trying to answer is why some countries and some regions develop more than others. I do not intend to devote space to a definition of 'development'. I take it to mean that people earn a better living through economic growth, which in this modern world inevitably involves change, adaptation and innovation. New technologies, new products and new forms of organisation are the very essence of growth, which just as inevitably generates conflict over who bears the costs and who reaps the benefits.

When we ask this big question, we often receive seemingly straightforward answers that on closer scrutiny prove incomplete and even contradictory. Many say that market magic has brought more development than has planning, but most economies are mixed. Consider cases like Japan and South Korea: both qualify as capitalistic and yet have industry policies that highlight the role of government. Others would stress differences in physical and human resources: fertile fields, great rivers and mountains of ore clearly make a difference. Surely culture plays its part and helps determine relative economic performance, if by culture we mean 'a living, historical product of group problem solving' (van Maanen and Barley 1985). There is, of course, policy as an explanatory factor. Some nations and regions seem to create their competitive edge by their own policies. They pick good prospects and ensure success by a mix of R & D, information provision, co-ordination and foreign marketing, offsetting disadvantages in physical resources and human capital.

Here we meet one of the more conspicuous failures of conventional economic analysis. Inequality in economic development among regions is not explicable by the axioms of conventional economics, which would try to explain the differences in per capita income by differences in physical and human resources per capita. This would seem to be quite inadequate, especially when trade and capital flows should do much to reduce income differences. This pushes us towards the conclusion that somehow the production possibilities differ: that given the same resources, more can be achieved in some regions than in others. Money capital flows readily enough in response to opportunities to make profit. However, information is not transmitted as readily. So we have to consider the costs of information, the value placed upon it, and the processes by which it is transmitted and put to use. In short, economic success depends upon informational efficiency.

This idea is no longer new; it derives from the now fully-fledged information economics (Lamberton 1984). I know the spectacular events portrayed in, for example, James Martin's *Technology's Crucible* (1987), have persuaded some to think that economics no longer has a role in this Information Age. I argue, however, that resource allocation problems remain and that it is a different economics that we need. The majority of economists, unaware of these frontier developments, or aware and either unappreciative of their significance or fearful of their consequences, reject the challenge and cling to the core of their discipline. In so doing they are missing exciting developments in that part of the universe of learning characterised by the keyword, *information* - not only information economics (including the economics of organisation, transactions cost economics and principal-agent theory) but also cognitive science, computer and information science, linguistics, cybernetics, communication sciences, informatics and even infometrics (Machlup and Mansfield 1983).

These developments have strong support from leading scholars. Stiglitz of Princeton University, formerly Drummond Professor at Oxford, places informational considerations as 'a central part of the Foundations of Economic Analysis', with information economics providing 'a new perspective, a new way of approaching Economic Analysis' that has 'cast doubt' on all fundamental maxims of traditional economic analysis (Stiglitz 1985). Differences in information - asymmetric information - form the centrepiece of his research programme, a programme said to provide 'an interesting and tractable route out of the macroeconomic wasteland of models based on *ad hoc* assumptions of market clearing or quantity constraints' (George and Sayer 1988). Weizsacker (1984), one of Europe's leading economists, goes so far as to say information economics is this generation's general framework for formulating any problems about efficient allocation of resources.

The concept of informational efficiency has much to contribute to the explanation of relative rates of economic growth. It is a concept that can help to reduce to some order the multiplicity of explanations of development; a concept that can explain the failure of conventional economics. Conventional economics fails because it assumes no constraints on man's information gathering, processing, communicating, deciding and agreeing-capabilities (Nelson 1981). In practice these constraints are formidable and it is fatal to assume optimal utilisation of information

Table 2.1 Typology of information occupations

- *Information producers*
  Scientific and technical workers
  Market search and co-ordination specialists
  Information gatherers
  Consultative services
- *Information processors*
  Administrative and managerial
  Process control and supervisory
  Clerical and related (components)
- *Information distributors*
  Educators
  Communication workers
- *Information infrastructure occupations*
  Information machine workers
  Postal and telecommunication

In real economics, information activities absorb a large share of national resources. We can lump them all together and refer to them as the quaternary or information sector. Table 2.1 provides a typology of information occupations: information producers, processors and distributors, along with those who operate the information infrastructure, for example the postal and telecommunication systems. The long-term historical trend in developed economies has been for an expansion of the information sector, with agriculture declining markedly and with deindustrialisation, that is a recorded contraction of industry. What seems to have gone largely unnoticed is that industry has become a greater user of information goods and services and that its decline is to some considerable extent a change in the nature of its activities - a structural shift from industry to the information sector. How big is the sector? In some countries, the information workforce is more than 40 per cent of the actively employed and, because of higher relative earnings, may account for more than 50 per cent of the wage bill.

Information-sector measurement and mapping have absorbed much of the efforts of information economists but they have addressed a wide range of matters. Some of the basic economic characteristics of information and information channels that have emerged are:

1. There is a great deal of difference between individual and group (or organisational) use of information. The division of information gathering may well be the most fundamental form of the division of labour. The gains must, however, be set against increased communication costs.
2. The cost of producing information is independent of the scale on which it is used.
3. The greater part of the cost of information is often the cost incurred by the recipient.
4. Learning takes time so that there is a limit to the rate at which decision-makers can absorb information.
5. There are usually significant information differentials in terms of possession of information, access to information and capability of using information.
6. The stock of information and the organisations created to handle information have the characteristics of capital.
7. The output of the information sector is used very largely by industry and commerce.
8. The demand for information equipment, for example computers and telephones, is a derived demand, dependent upon the demand for computations performed and information transmitted.
9. The actual combination of economic characteristics is such that the successful pursuit of efficiency can lead to organisational obsolescence.

Table 2.2 links the sector and the developed process. It uses an alternative measure for the primary information sector; the percentage of all goods and services sold that can be regarded as information goods and services, for example newspapers, advertising services, education, communication. Developed economies are high on the list. We should not, however, jump to the conclusion that a large information sector will ensure development. Informational efficiency is very clearly dependent upon what happens in the information sector - upon the kinds of information goods and services produced and how they are used. Much of the information sector output is normally purchased by business and government. When this supply of important business services is not available, we should not expect good development performance. There is a secondary information sector that is made up from the same sorts of goods and services produced in-house and *not* sold on markets. Quantitatively, this secondary sector may be as large as the primary sector, and its proper functioning may be of crucial importance for informational efficiency.

Table 2.2. Primary information sectors: % GDP (factor cost)

1970s*

	(%)
Australia	36
United States	24
Singapore	24
United Kingdom	22
France	19
Japan	19
New Zealand	19
Sweden	17
Malaysia	16
Fiji	15
Philippines	13
Papua New Guinea	11
Venezuela	10
Thailand	10

Source: OECD 1986; Jussawalla *et al* 1988; for Venezuela, M. Rubin (personal communication).

*N.B. Data do not relate to the same year so furnish only a broad comparison.

To date, the information economics armoury has not been much used in addressing regional matters. While information-sector studies have been extended from OECD countries to less-developed countries like Indonesia, Malaysia, Thailand, Papua New Guinea and Fiji (Jussawalla 1988), not much has been done to measure and map the regional sectors. I appreciate that there are problems with the information sector approach, as with input/output analysis itself. Nevertheless, it seems a promising route to follow. We should not despair if we do not get spectacular results immediately. One can take heart from that great pioneer of national income analysis, Colin Clark, now in his retirement. Much has been achieved during the span of his distinguished career.

So let us look to see if, as Weld suggested, the very differences are illuminating. Taking the primary-information-sector measures in Table 2.2, Australia at 36 per cent heads the list; Venezuela and Thailand are at the bottom with 10 per cent. We need to go on to examine the structural relationships. Is there a resonable balance between routine and creative activities? Is search underway for new markets and new products? Is the new information capital - telecommunications, computers and human skills - available? If that capital is available, is it being used? Is there evidence of organisational adaptation as new technology is introduced?

For these purposes both national and regional information-sector accounts need to be supplemented by detailed statistics of information activity. Ideally, a complete system of information flows paralleling that of the real processes can be conceptualised. Collecting and maintaining such statistics are, of course, costly, and selective development of indicators may be all that is practicable. To date, at both national and regional levels greatest attention has been given to media and postal and telecommunication activity. However, 'the dominant resource-using activity in an economy - the processing, interpretation and intermediation of information' (Eliasson 1987), permeates business, government and non-profit organisations. Hence a more comprehensive range of indices is needed in the interest of general efficiency and to enable detection of significant differences amongst nations and regions.

By taking account of differences in information (i.e. asymmetric information), economists have, I believe, made significant advances in the analysis of individual markets and of the macroeconomic working of the economy. An interesting recent illustration is the modification of the Dornbusch theory of exchange rates suggested by Goodhart (1988). By distinguishing different groups of buyers and sellers of currencies, each drawing on a different set of information, Goodhart has modified the Dornbusch theory to give better predictions and has opened up a new line of research. In that he is now committed to trying to explain how changes in the balance of power between his group come about, he has raised a matter of quite general interest and one that certainly has application in the regional context.

We can treat the information asymmetries in a simple fashion: A knows and B does not know. However, the asymmetries can also be regarded as a consequence of differential rates of learning, and of differential efficiencies in communication processes ranging from face-to-face communication between individuals, through education and broadcasting, to the operation of highly computerised capital-intensive management information systems. Analytically, we need to replace the simple assumption about what A and B know with some more complex but still manageable assumptions about a communication process. In other words, we need to put some theory of learning into economics.

This will lead us into consideration of our institutions - the information handling organisations usually taken as given by economists. As the director of the imaginative and ambitious UK ESRC PICT (Economic and Social Research Council Programme on Information & Communication Technologies) reasons:

> Technologically advanced countries have grown increasingly dependent upon electronic information and communication systems. Most of their institutions have been structured around these systems. Explanations of the functions and effects of these institutions are premised upon (often implicit) assumptions about the state of underlying information and communication networks. When these networks undergo major changes, many explanations of economic and social phenomena developed from the study of the old order are reduced in significance or rendered obsolete. Uncertainty is increased. The new information and communication systems are often more complex than the old. Understanding is more difficult to obtain, yet more important to pursue. Ironically, in our age where information and communication systems are more sophisticated and comprehensive than ever before, the planning horizons for decision makers of all kinds are continuously being reduced because of a growing inability to forecast even short-term future developments. Seldom in our history has a subject attracted such attention, yet yielded so little critical insight into its long-term future developments. (Melody 1987)

Institutions do matter. When we try to change or invent them, we must look closely at the information conditions that shape them. This applies with special force to regional institutions. Isard (1987) points out that 'The very latest probings (by regional scientists) concern the development of appropriate information and data management systems for multi-region entities, [and] investment in information generation to reduce uncertainty in all kinds of decisions'. Because regional development rests inevitably on specialisation, a region needs to co-ordinate its activities with those of other regions, both within its nation and externally. In view of the proliferation of supranational institutions that we have witnessed in modern times (Wolfe 1977), I venture to suggest that successful endogenous regional development will generate a similar supraregional proliferation. Such new institutions cater for real needs, but the benefits must be balanced against their costs. The pressures for their creation will stem, in part, from efforts to remove the informational inefficiencies inherent in the accidental nature of regional boundaries.

In conclusion, let me return to my initial indictment of the computer age. Why have the expected gains from massive investment in intelligent electronics not shown up in the productivity statistics? What lessons are there when we seek to promote regional development? I admit readily that there are problems in measuring productivity, but I believe there are other reasons that must be taken into account in efforts to build regional initiatives on the exploitation of information resources.

1. *Capital concept*: All too often capital is thought of as machines and buildings. It is not appreciated that expenditure on information is investment in capital. So too is the creation of organisational capability to enquire, communicate, decide.
2. *Accounting methods:* Information is not treated as a line item. We need better bookkeeping in the information economy. When labour and raw materials dominated costs, a small balance of fixed costs that included information costs could be apportioned on the basis of those variable costs. Now we have what *The Economist* 1987 has called 'Upside-down accounting'. If information costs are the greater part of the total, we need a modern accounting to guide investment in information as well as investment in machines and buildings. This is a necessary step towards achieving informational efficiency.
3. *Import requirements:* There appears to be a failure to make adequate allowance for the import bill involved in becoming a modern, hi-tech information economy. Let me use my own country as an illustration. Through 1981-6 exports by the information industries remained flat around $Aust. 0.1 billion, while the corresponding imports mounted from $1.3 billion to $3.4 billion. At present the gap is over $4 billion a year and the official forecast is $10 billion by the early 1990s (*Australian Technology Magazine* 1987).
4. *Competitive advantage is a race:* Creating and holding competitive advantage is a race. It is necessary to pick the race for which the region is best suited and then train for that event. A great deal depends on the process by which the new technologies that are to be the basis of regional specialisation are selected. Full exploitation of

> information resources would ensure that the information yielded by thorough social and economic evaluation of technological prorities is highly valued. Perhaps the most difficult task of all is staying in front in the race because the very characteristics of information that initially create opportunities can, in the course of time, put the brakes on. The combination of uncertainty, indivisibility and capital intensity generate reliance upon the existing information sources and a high-risk attitude towards new proposals. We know too little about ways of keeping organisations permanently young and permanently innovative.

A fundamental structural change has taken place and it affects all economies. Acquiring new skills in the management of information resources, designing of new forms of organisation, and shaping new information policy have become necessary but interdependent steps in economic growth. However, the Information Age gives no guarantee that all countries and all regions will develop. The most successful will no doubt be those that foster creativity, learn to manage their information resources, pick some winners and indulge in some protectionism. They will, I believe, be countries or regions that have accorded priority to social science research into the information economy. Even then their rewards will not come quickly. The capabilities to which I have been referring grow slowly and the quick solution can prove very costly. It is a race; but Charles Carter, economist and academic administrator, probably got it right when he gave the advice to 'Be a beetle not a kangaroo', if you seek success in economic development.

References

Australian Technology Magazine (1987) Special Edition: An information industries strategy, September.

The Economist (1987) 'Factory of the future: a survey'. 30 May.

George, D. A., and Sayer, S. (1988) Econometric Society European Meeting 1987, *Journal of Economic Surveys* 2(1): 97-101.

Goodhart, C. (1988) 'Why is the dollar so stable?' *The Economist*, 9, April 1988. PP. 3-18

Eliasson, G. (1987) 'The economics of institutions and markets' in *IUI 1987 Yearbook 1986-1987*. Stockholm: Industrial Institute for Economic and Social Research.

Isard, W. (1987) 'Regional science: retrospect and prospect: an interview with Walter Isard'. *Regional Science* 39(2): 153-8.

Jussawalla, M., Lamberton, D. M., and Karunaratne, N. D. (eds.) (1988) *The Cost of Thinking: Information Economies of Ten Pacific Countries*. Norwood, NJ: Ablex Publishing.

Lamberton, D. M. (1984) 'The economics of information and organisation', in Williams, M. E. (ed.) *Annual Review of Information Science and Technology* (ARIST), 19, American Society for Information Science.

Machlup, F. and Mansfield, U. (eds.) (1983) *The Study of Information: Interdisciplinary Messages*. New York: John Wiley.

Martin, J. (1987) *Technology's Crucible: An Exploration of the Explosive Impact of Technology on Society during the Next Four Decades*. Englewood Cliffs, NJ: Prentice-Hall.

Melody, W. H. (1987) 'UK research on implications of information and communication technologies'. *Telecommunications Policy* 11(1): 11-19.

Nelson, R. R. (1981) 'Assessing private enterprise: an exegesis of tangled doctrine'. *Bell Journal of Economics* 12(1): 93-111.

OECD (1986) *Trends in the Information Economy*. Paris, OECD.

Solow, R. (1987) Review of S. S. Cohen and J. Zysman, *Manufacturing Matters: The Myth of the Post Industrial Economy*. New York Times Book Review 36 (12 July).

Stiglitz, J. E. (1985) 'Information and economic analysis: a perspective'. *Economic Journal*, Supplement to vol. 95: 21-41.

Maanen, J. van , and Barley, S. R. (1985) 'Cultural organisation: fragments of a theory', in P.J. Frost, *et al.* (eds.) *Organisational Culture*. London: Sage Publications.

Weizsacker, C. C. von (1984) 'The cost of substitution' *Econometrica* 52(5): 1085-116.

Weld, W. E. (1924) 'Regional comparison and economic progress', in R. G. Tugwell (ed.) *The Trend of Economics*. New York: Alfred A. Knopf.

Wolfe, A. W. (1977) 'The supranational organisation of production: an evolutionary perspective'. *Current Anthropology* 18(4): 615-35.

3. Geographical advantage in the information economy

Mark E. Hepworth

Centre for Urban and Regional Development Studies
University of Newcastle upon Tyne

As we all know, geographical advantage in the information economy is a contingent relation. It depends on the locational calculus of firms - for example, why, how and where should a head office be established? It is also conditioned by the decisions of governments - for example, which regions need extra support in telecommunications? And, in both cases, we need to account for the passage of time. By this I mean taking account of the historical geography of the information economy, as well as monitoring the recent course of developments.

Reflecting the logic of these opening remarks, I begin with some historical referencing of the information economy and its attendant geography. I follow this with a brief overview of two recent developments which have revealed and highlighted the centrality of information in the economy: the so called 'information technology revolution' of course, and, the global 'cloud of uncertainty' (incomplete information) which presently hovers over business and government decisions. I then present some tentative observations on the geographical implications of these most recent developments, with respect to the interregional distribution of production and market institutions. My concluding remarks take us back to the notion of 'geographical advantage' in the information economy.

The secular growth of the information economy

In his recent book, *The Control Revolution* , James Beniger (1986) traces the economic and technological origins of the Information Society in America to the second half of the nineteenth century. His historical analysis reveals a steady development of organisational, information-processing and communication technology in the wake of the Industrial Revolution and prior to the Second World War. These developments include, in particular, the appearance of telecommunications and computer innovations and the rise of private and public bureaucracies as control technologies. In common with Charles Jonscher (1983) and Daniel Bell (1973), Beniger attributes the historical growth of the information economy to the spiralling control requirements of mass production, mass distribution and mass consumption. Indeed, he suggests that the organisational basis of the information economy - the control hierarchies of large corporations and central government - and their technological structure were firmly established not during or after the Second World War but before 1939. The post-war period, then, has basically witnessed the consolidation of these organisational forms and technological structures, as expressed by the multinational corporation, the Keynesian or welfare state and the vastly expanded complex of electronic information and communication industries.

The general effects of these secular trends on the economic base of industrialised countries were first noted by Fritz Machlup (1962), and later they were more thoroughly codified and measured by Marc Porat (1977). The latter's methodology is now used as a basis for the OECD's international studies (OECD 1985). And, according to the OECD's evidence, advanced economies passed a significant 'threshold' in the last two decades to become 'information economies'. The supporting facts are that, in these economies, the bulk of the labour force is engaged in informational activities and the bulk of wealth is generated from information goods and services.

My own research has focused on the regional geography of the information economy within individual countries. The evidence I have collected relates specifically to Canada and the United Kingdom. It clearly shows that, in both of these countries, the information economy is unevenly developed in a geographical sense. For example, in Canada for 1981, over 50 per cent of the province of Ontario's labour force worked in information occupation, but this figure was less than 40 per cent in the province of Newfoundland. By way of comparison, in Britain for the same year, information occupations made up 47 per cent of the South East region's workforce, but only 38 per cent of the regional workforce in Northern England (Hepworth 1986, 1987).

Clearly, there is a historical explanation for these patterns of uneven regional development which, as Beniger suggests, originate in the nineteenth century. I would, therefore, attribute this development trajectory to the historical geography of large corporations and central government in both countries. This view is consistent with the influential work of Allan Pred (1977), who explains the spatial bias of the information economy in terms of the mutually reinforcing effects of corporate and urban-regional hierarchies. A primary focus of this research has been the location of head office (hierarchies) and their horizontal linkages with local information industries (markets) (Gottmann 1983). More generally, regional development in the information economy has been examined in relation to the local architectures of these hierarchies and markets and their differential and cumulative effects. This applies, for example, to the interregional diffusion of research and development, the geographical expansion of advanced telecommunications, or the differential decision-making capacities of private- and public-sector institutions.

In sum, recent developments in the information economy are not occurring on a blank spatial surface; rather, they are conditioned by the historical geography of capitalist economic development, with its dominant structures of corporate and government hierarchies. Let us now turn to these recent developments in the information economy.

Uncertainty and the information technology revolution

First, the technological revolution. To cut a long story short, I agree with the leading experts, such as Christopher Freeman (1984), who see the new electronic generation of information technology as providing a propulsive force for the next long wave of capitalist economic development - the so-called Fifth Kondratieff Cycle.

Importantly, as product and process innovations, the profound impacts of the new technology evince the central role of information in the economy (Lamberton 1982). This holds true for the world's 24-hour financial markets, as much as it does for the small manufacturing firm using computerised production techniques.

The second broad development which has lately magnified the value of information, is the higher level of uncertainty in the global economy. In their influential book *The Second Industrial Divide*, Piore and Sabel (1984) attribute this uncertain environment to the destablishing effects on industrialised countries and American industry in particular, of a succession of economic implosions through the 1970s. The supply-side factors, they identify, are declining labour productivity, high interest rates, high energy prices, Third World competition in standardised manufactures and the switch from fixed to flexible exchange rates; on the demand side, Piore and Sabel point to the saturation of consumer markets and the recessionary effects of national budgetary policies, which sought to mitigate balance-of-payments pressures through fiscal and monetary restraint.

According to Piore and Sabel, whose work is partly inspired by the French regulation school of political economy (Aglietta 1979), we are witnessing a crisis in Fordist institutions. This refers not only to the Fortune 500 companies, with their unwieldy bureaucracies and rigid, assembly-line techniques of mass production based on a highly codified division of labour, but also to the post-war Keynesian state with its dual capacity for guaranteeing effective demand and a minimum social wage, on which mass consumer markets depend.

Against this background of crisis or loss of control at the microeconomic and macroeconomic levels, firms have grown more reliant on information and the new information technology, as a basis for flexible adjustment to environmental uncertainty. As stated by Arrow:

> When there is uncertainty, risk aversion implies that steps will be taken to reduce risks. This partly affects decisions within the firm, such as the holding of inventories and preference for flexible capital equipment, and partly leads to new markets which will shift risks to those most able and willing to bear them, particularly through the equity market. (Arrow 1984)

Indeed, over the last years, we have seen clear signs of this risk-shifting, or the decentralisation of economic activities from corporate hierarchies to market (Williamson 1975). This applies to both the labour and the capital market, as indicated respectively by the growth of so-called flexible working and popular share ownership, and also to vertical disintegration in product markets, as marked by the growth of subcontracting among firms.

At the same time, the use of computer network technology, both as wide area and local area systems, enabled firms to alter radically the informational parameters of production, consumption and management processes - not only at individual operating sites but also at the organisational and inter-organisational levels. Arising from these innovations, as new technologies for control and functional integration, are all manner of information-based, flexible arrangements in the firm and in the economy :

1. Flexible production lines that generate a familial variety of commodities, based on economies of scope in the use of capital (multi-application machines) and labour (multi-task workers);
2. Flexible specialisation in territorial production complexes, based on external economies of scale flowing from a highly articulated inter-firm division of labour;
3. Flexible consumption systems, based on the self-service principle, such as so called home-banking and tele-shopping;

4. Flexible corporations, marked by what Drucker (1988) calls the information-based organisation, and which he likens to the symphony orchestra owing to its peculiar composition of musical (knowledge) specialists.

What I am referring to, then, is the changing industrial organisation of the information economy. The general significance of these changes is, of course, that they challenge and potentially overturn the rigid hierarchical structures of the information economy I described earlier. Let us now return to the question of regional geography: first, to the information space of production and, second, to the information space of market-making institutions.

The information space of production

The spatial dynamics of the information economy, particulary its recent expresssion, has become a central concern in geographical research. Consider, for example, this comment by Manuel Castells :

> The current process of technological change is characterised, as everybody knows, by the fact that it represents a new form of production, based on information and knowledge as the major sources of productivity. Yet, its development is taking place within the existing modes of production (capitalism and statism) whose logic it tends to reinforce.
>
> (Castells 1987)

In fact, with the deepening of the information economy in manufacturing industry, there is a noticeable blurring of the lines of analytical (and professional) interest which have traditionally divided economic geographers into two main camps - manufacturing versus services. These internal barriers, unfortunately, remain and have contributed to the declaration of new discoveries by industrial geographers - such as flexible specialisation and the agglomerative effects of market information - although these same discoveries have a long history in the material economy and in geographical research, particularly in urban and service sector studies (Gertler 1988). For the sake of simplicity, however, I will summarise the state of the art as it now appears in the geographical literature. The dominant themes, as I see them, are economic decentralisation (from hierarchies to markets) and spatial decentralisation (from core to periphery), and their interrelatedness.

First, let us look at the new service economy (Gershuny and Miles 1983). Here, the evidence on regional change appears to be reducible to two broad developments. First, information services are still geographically distributed along hierarchical lines, with head offices and producer services (e.g. finance and advertising) remaining concentrated in dominant urban regions; however, there is some evidence of the break-up of corporate and government bureaucracies, with routine or back office information services decentralising to so called peripheral regions (Noyelle 1987). Second, there is the internationalisation of certain information services, particularly through foreign direct investment (e.g. finance, accounting and public data service) (Howells 1988); so far, these globalisation trends have worked in favour of what Friedmann and Wolff (1982) call world cities - such as the European capitals, New York and Tokyo.

Now, what of manufacturing production? A great source of interest here is what the space economy will look like after Fordism? For some geographers, like Allen Scott (1988), we are likely to see 'The rise of new industrial spaces in North America and Europe'. These new spaces of so-called flexible specialisation, it is envisaged, will be comprised of territorial production complexes, wherein small innovative firms are bound together by technological complementarities and the need to exchange information intensively on markets and production. In some existing cases these new complexes have developed around older industrial areas, owing to their information-dependent, subcontracting relations with large manufacturing firms (a dependency reinforced by the use of just-in-time systems). Other complexes have, however, evolved in the newly-industrialised, Sunbelt regions of Europe and the United States, where so-called technopoles and non-unionised manufacturing plants flourish in fine weather conditions.

The great attraction of flexible specialisation complexes is, of course, their promise of a return to the old days - the more democratic landscape of the nineteenth-century Marshallian industrial districts. But, the probability of economic history repeating itself is not really calculable from the evidence advanced thus far. All we have, at the moment, is the reporting of isolated examples: the Hollywood movie industry, the Silicon Valley technopoles and, of course, the New Italy. We will clearly have to wait and see whether these are harbingers of a new type of regional economy or merely 'candles in the wind'.

My own research, conducted largely in Canada, has focused not on spatially contiguous production complexes or particular regional economies, but on the general spatial implications of private computer networking in large companies. The case studies, which I have carried out, cover several different sectors of the economy, including services and manufacturing (Hepworth 1987). What I have found is that computer network technologies enable large firms to achieve the following :

1. Centralised and decentralised spatial arrangements of both office and manufacturing production activity at a larger geographical scale.
2. Highly complex spatial divisions of labour, enabled by enhanced central control over spatially decentralised and occupationally-differentiated work processes.
3. Expanded market geographies for products and services, including the penetration of new regional and international markets, enabled by the central provision of capital services to scaled-down branch establishments and transborder data flows that evade national tariff barriers; and
4. The enlargement of information space which bounds locational, investment and other management decision-making, through the intelligence-gathering of extensive branch networks, the purchase of on-line political and economic information from public data bases and real time monitoring of transactions at the organisational level.

What I think is emerging from all this disparate and albeit limited evidence is not so much a clear image of a new regional economy, but, perhaps just as significantly, a timely questioning of the characteristic hierarchical structure of the information economy's geography. The 'devil in the piece', so to speak, is what I refer to as the communicability of information capital - that is, the circulation of capital services embodied in information flowing within and between operations sites, and over local area and wide area computer networks (Hepworth and Waterson 1988). It is these information flows, whether in the flexible factory or in the flexible financial market, which we must examine rigorously in order to develop an appropriate theoretical and empirical basis for future regional policy. Not only do they impinge on production and management structures, through their functionally-differentiated effects on economies of scale and scope, but also these information flows affect the allocation of economic activity between hierarchies and markets, through their alteration of transactions costs and their distribution between firms, governments and individual workers and consumers.

The information space of market institutions

So far, I have discussed only production space. But this is not all of the information economy: we must also look at the institutional fabric of markets, which after all are the information systems which serve to allocate resources in the economy, including their geographical distribution. Indeed, I have discussed regional development in the information economy - and implicitly, the question of 'geographical advantage' - in terms of the balance of markets and hierarchies in a spatial context.

This is an altogether more difficult task to address, as Arrow (1984) implies: 'The market is a much more ethereal construct. Who exactly is it that is achieving the balance of supply and demand? Where in fact is the information on bids and offers needed for equilibration actually collected and stored?' In fact, it is clear that much of the information economy consists of 'making markets'. This includes not only in-house corporate activities - such as advertising, sales and purchases and market research - but also an entire array of information industries, such as publishing and the on-line industry, and industry, market and other specialised associations. Additional to these private sector institutions are, of course, the various levels of government, from the central regulators of competition in markets to the local regulators of urban land use and the branch offices that monitor local labour markets.

It is obvious that the refashioning of old markets and the creation of new ones cannot go forward without information. At least in Britain this is happening in a number of different but related contexts. First, there is the internationalisation of markets, including the consolidation of the EEC in 1992. These developments have generated a bonanza for the information industries, including university-based experts, the media and the law and accountancy firms, as much as they have revitalised government bureaucracies, not just in Brussels but in the different national civil services where the minute details of market harmonisation have to be carefully worked out.

Within Britain, and apparently in other European countries, there is the information business created out of so called deregulation - a line of business which of course is already big in the United States. As Loasby (1976) notes, 'competition implies ignorance, as non-economists have always believed: competition is not a state of equilibrium but a process of search'. Importantly, for our consideration of geography, old information is public, spatially concentrated and is to be easily found in the publications, files and archives of bureaucracies; but new information is private, dispersed throughout the space economy and it needs to be retrieved from individual firms and consumers, if new markets are to be established at all.

The general implication of market-making, on the grand scale of economy-wide deregulation, EEC consolidation or comprehensive informatics planning, is that new market-minded institutions have to be created at the regional or local level. This may involve governments acting as market information brokers, the creation of enterprise agencies, the wholesaling of work gangs and greater stringency in the allocation of welfare benefits, the generalised cut-back of public sector services, and the multiplication of market-related decision-making capacity in the branch plants and offices of manufacturing firms, banks and other large multilocational organisations.

Conclusion

So, what of geographical advantage in the information economy - the title of my chapter? My basic message is that, if regional policy is not to generate a succession of white elephants through misdirected public expenditures, we must first develop a better understanding of the information economy and its spatial behaviour and expression. As such, I will not conclude with the usual list of antidotes for regional development problems - say, eighteen-hole golf courses for 'high-tech' executives and ISDNs for farming economies - but, instead, I will finish on a more whimsical note. It consists of three questions: Will geography really matter in the year 2000, when the information economy is fully networked? What will take its place? And finally, who cares anyway?

References

Aglietta, M. (1979) *A Theory of Capitalist Regulation: The US Experience*. London: New Left Books.

Arrow, K. J. (1984) *The Economics of Information (Collected Papers)*. Cambridge, Mass: The Belknap Press of Harvard University.

Bell, D. (1973) *The Coming of Post-industrial Society*. Basic Books, New York.

Beniger, J. (1986) *The Control Revolution: Technological and Economic Origins of the Information Society*. Cambridge, Mass: Harvard University Press.

Castells, M. (1987) 'Technological change, economic restructuring and the spatial division of labour', in H. Muegge, W. Stohr, P. Hesp and B. Stuckey (eds.) *International Economic Restructuring and the Regional Community*. Aldershot: Gower Press.

Drucker, P. (1988) 'The coming of the new organisation'. *Harvard Business Review* January-February.

Freeman, C. (1984) *The Role of Technical Change in National Economic Development*. Science Policy Research Unit, Sussex University. Mimeo.

Friedmann, J, and Wolff, G. (1982) 'World city formation : an agenda for research and action'. *International Journal for Urban and Regional Research* 6: 307-43.

Gershuny, J., and Miles, I. (1983). *The New Service Economy*. London: Frances Pinter.

Gertler, M. (1988). 'The limits to flexibility : comments on the post-Fordist vision of production and its geography'. Paper presented at the Annual Meeting of the Association of American Geographers, Phoenix, Arizona, 8 April.

Gottmann, J. (1983) *The Coming of the Transactional City.* Institute for Urban Studies, University of Maryland.
Hepworth, M. (1986) 'The geography of technological change in the information economy'. *Regional Studies;* (with Green, A. and Gillespie, A.), 'The spatial division of information labour in Great Britain'. *Environment and Planning A*, 19, 1987, 793-806.
Hepworth, M. (1987). 'The geography of the information economy'. Unpublished P D. dissertation, University of Toronto.
Hepworth, M. and Waterson, M. (1988). 'Information technology and the spatial dynamics of capital. *Information Economics and Policy* (forthcoming).
Howells, J. (1988) *Economic Technological and Locational Trends in European Services.* Aldershot, Gower Press.
Johnscher, C. (1983) 'Information resources and economic productivity'. *Information Economics and Policy* 1(1), 13-35.
Lamberton, D. (1982) 'The theoretical implications of measuring the communications sector', in Jussawalla, M., and Lamberton, D. (eds), *Communications Economics and Development.* New York: Pergamon.
Loasby, B. (1976) *Choice, Complexity and Ignorance.* Cambridge: Cambridge University Press.
Machlup, F. (1962) *The Production and Distribution of Knowledge in the United States.* Princeton, NJ: Princeton University Press.
Noyelle, T. (1987) *The Shift to Service Economy.* London: Frances Pinter.
OECD (1985) *Update of Information Sector Statistics.* ICCP Committee Report. Paris: OECD.
Porat, M. (1977) *The Information Economy: Definition and Measurement.* US Department of Commerce, Washington DC, Office of Telecommunication Special Publication 72-12(1).
Piore, M., and Sabel, F. (1984) *The Second Industrial Divide.* New York: Basic Books.
Pred, A. (1977). *City Systems in Advanced Economies.* New York: Wiley.
Scott, A. (1988) 'Flexible production systems and regional development'. *International Journal of Urban and Regional Research.* (forthcoming).
Williamson, O. (1975) *Markets and Hierarchies: Analysis and Anti-trust Implications.* New York: The Free Press.

4. Mobilising invisible assets: the key for successful corporate strategy

Hiroyuki Itami

Professor of Management
Faculty of Commerce
Hitotsubashi University
Kunitachi, Toyko, Japan

The focus of this paper is a very simple concept and the power of a simple concept as a means of understanding the successful long-term growth of a firm. It is relevant to the growth of a firm in any age but particularly in the information technology age.

The basic concept is that of invisible assets and underlying this, that of information flow. These concepts cannot be sufficiently stressed. As Professor Lamberton has discussed, economists have traditionally thought of capital as materials, money and machines - the visible things. Observation over a considerable period of successes and failures of many Japanese firms has however convinced me that the real competitive edge does not come from the physical and visible resources. It comes from those things which we cluster together as intangible resources or invisible assets. They are information-based assets, and this is why a small but growing number of managers are adding information to the economists' list of the capital inputs to the productive process. Obviously all resources are necessary for a business, but one must distinguish two kinds of necessity. Some resources, for example the plant, must be physically present for business operations to take place. Others are necessary for competitive success. Most physical and monetary assets and some human are necessary in the first sense. Most invisible assets and some human resources are necessary in this second sense. The purpose of this chapter is to provide a conceptual framework within which the role of the information-based invisible assets can be better understood and therefore better managed.

Concrete examples of successful corporate strategies help to introduce what otherwise might appear to be an abstract discussion. The successful introduction of a new product onto the market brings out a number of points.

IBM succeeded in introducing its personal computer when the market was actually occupied by Apple and other smaller firms. Similarly, Sony successfully introduced a compact receiver and headphone set for simultaneous translation at meetings and conferences. Two questions arise. First, why were they successful? Why did they succeed in introducing these new products to the market. Second, what gains and benefits did successes bring to these firms?

In thinking about reasons behind its success, one wonders whether IBM succeeded because of its visible assets. For example, did IBM succeed in its development and monitoring of the PC because it had factories or because it had money? The answer must be that IBM succeeded because it had the technological skill, brand names, distribution channels and large networks. The same is true for Sony. Sony succeeded in developing this translation equipment not because they had factories or money or labour, but because they had technological skill, brand names, information on the customers' needs, or a good corporate culture which entails being very responsive to the needs of customers.

The same can be said for the gains from the successes. IBM's gain from success in the PC business included money, but this was not the most important thing that they got. They created a new image for IBM, they created technological skills in a different line of business from mainframe computers, and they created a new corporate culture. *Business Week* by saying in a cover story some years ago that the PC changed the way that IBM thinks, perceived clearly a change in corporate culture brought about by the success in introducing the PC.

Technological skills, brand names, corporate culture, distribution channels, these are intangibles, the invisible assets of a firm. They are both the reasons behind success and the true gains from success, gains which will be meaningful for the long-term future of the firm. Money, turnover and profit, was not significant in this respect.

What are invisible assets? Table 4.1 set out in three groups those things which I consider to be invisible assets. Because they are intangible, unlike money or buildings or equipment, they are difficult to grasp as assets. They are very diverse and do not appear to fit easily with one another. There is however one way to conceptualise them in a single, unified framework, and this framework is called the information flow. This is my basic and very simple thesis - all invisible assets are based on one kind of information flow or another. For example, accumulated customer information is very valuable in developing the right kind of product for the right kind of market at the right time. It is information accumulated within the firm about the environment, in this case that part of the environment which is the market. It is a stock of information which the firm has accumulated because of the information flow from the environment into the firm resulting from learning activities such as marketing or servicing of customers.

Table 4.1 Types of information

A. Accumulated customer information
Technological know-how and skills
Distribution channels
Customer networks
B. Brand names
Reputation
Advertising know-how
Marketing know-how
C. Corporate culture
Managerial skills
International management

Environmental information flows from the environment to the firm create invisible assets related to the environment and these assets include not only technological skills, production know-how and customer information - the accumulated stock of information - they also include the channels and the capacity of these channels for bringing in information.

Technology is information accumulated within the firm about nature and how nature functions. When two materials are brought together, in chemical reaction, a certain product will result. That is the way that nature functions. Human beings try to understand how nature functions and thus form a body of knowledge which is useful for production and other purposes. This is called technology. Research and development are information-gathering activities which in producing a flow of information add to the invisible asset base of the firm.

The technological skills of people within the firm also result from information flows between the environment and the firm. They are information acquired by the firm's engineers and workers on how machines and materials function. In learning how to use a machine or to programme software, or how to carry out other human activities, information flows into and is stored within the firm through its' people's minds. It thus becomes a valuable asset for the firm.

The second group of invisible assets listed in Table 4.1 involve a different kind of information flow. This is corporate information which is concerned with meaningful flows from the firm into the environment. Corporate information includes reputation, brand names, corporate image, influence over the distribution channel and over suppliers of parts as well as actual marketing know-how. The reason why a firm has an asset called a brand name is because of the good information which customers or consumers receive about the firm's product or service. Those people who work in Olivetti or Sony, for example, can have all kinds of good images about their firm, but this does not give value in the market. The good image has to be in the customer's mind. It is information concerning the firm, flowing into the environment, which makes the environment treat you better in a preferential way. In other words, once favourable information is accumulated by the firm's customers, they start preferring the firm's products over the competitors'. In much the same way, the firm's reputation is developed and functions with its suppliers and financiers. As with environmental information, it is not only the stock of information in the minds of customers, it is also the firm's ability and the capacity of its information channels to transmit the information effectively, as for example strong ties with retailers allied with experience in advertising.

The third group of invisible assets in Table 4.1 are concerned with internal information and internal information flows. It is information which originates and terminates within the firm. It includes corporate culture, managerial skills, morale of the workforce, as well as the firm's ability to manage information, its people's ability to transmit and use information in decision-making and in their operational tasks. Corporate culture is dominant in this group.

The firm is an organisation made up of people who exchange information, communicate with each other and either store this information or tell someone else about something which they think is important. The effectiveness of this process is highly dependent on the corporate culture. In the framework of information flows one can define corporate culture as the distinctive characteristics of the patterns of information processing shared by the members of an organisation.

For example, how would one characterise a firm which is said to have a very technology-oriented culture using this framework? I would describe it as an organisation in which people are very quickly responsive to technological information, even to the neglect of market-related information. They react well to it and quickly communicate to other people in the organisation in a very easy and cost-effective manner. They remember it well. There can be other descriptions of corporate culture such as market-oriented culture. Thinking in this framework however enables one to understand that corporate culture is a result of information flow within the firm, and of making it a habit for people to process information in a certain way.

Each of the three groups of invisible assets is related to one of three kinds of information flow. Emphasis must therefore again be not only on the accumulated stock of information in the firm but also on the information channels themselves. Hence, distribution networks are listed amongst the invisible assets, and it is the capacity of these information or communication networks which makes them effective and valuable. There is also an interdependency. Information received from the environment must not only be stored within the firm, it has to be transmitted to appropriate decision-makers quickly and accurately. An internal information flow system is essential. Without it, accumulated information has no value. It has to be used in strategic and other decisions.

The reason why I have focused on invisible assets and the information flows behind them and emphasise their importance is that I think that they are the only source of long-term competitive edge for the firm. Someone might respond by wondering, 'But how about money? how about physical resources?'

Let us take as an example the competitive edge of a painter, his talent as an artist which gives value to a painting. Of course, he must have some money to buy canvas, brushes, paints and other materials. He must also be physically present in order to paint the picture. These are not enough to create a masterpiece. Otherwise, even I could be a great master.

The reason why a painter has a competitive edge over others, perhaps a rather awful phrase to use of an artist, is because of his artistic sense, the invisible things inside him and behind him. It is necessary to have money and physical resources, but it is not enough. It is only the invisible resources which determine the competitiveness of an artist and a firm.

There are four key reasons why invisible assets are the only real source of competitive advantage. First, most of them cannot be readily bought in the market-place. There is no easy way to obtain a well-known brand name or advanced technological production skills in the market. Each firm must build up its own invisible assets. If money were the key then the Banco de Bilbao or Barclay's Bank would be a top computer manufacturer or a successful manufacturer of other kinds of products. They cannot be competitive as a manufacturer not only because they cannot buy the technological skills and other intangibles easily in the market-place but above all because they have not built-up an appropriate corporate culture. That cannot be bought off the shelf. Hence a firm differentiates itself from its competitors through its invisible assets. The resources embodied in invisible assets can be neither readily bought nor readily imitated. Accumulation of invisible assets takes time, and time is the second reason why these assets are the only source of competitive edge. They require on-going, conscious and time-consuming efforts. Competitors do not have easy access to them. Imitation takes time, and it takes a competitor even longer to build his own distinctive technological skills, brand, corporate culture, knowledge of customers and the customers' image of the firm.

The third reason why invisible assets are the source of competitive edge is that they allow you simultaneous multiple use. They give you a free ride because they are information based. They are thus a very efficient kind of resource. Sony, for example, can use the same brand name for TV, translation equipment, audio equipment, video cassette recorders and many other products at the same time. Sony may have built the brand name by its TV sets, but it can now use that brand name on other products without reducing its value for TVs. Honda deliberately exploited the reputation which it had built for quality in its cars and motorcycles to sell its lawnmowers. The slogan of its advertising campaign was 'Put a second Honda in your garage'. But this followed its successful multiple exploitation of its technology. It used its technology in small gas engines sequentially, first developed in motorcycles, it then applied the technology in cars, and then in lawnmowers, generators and outboard engines.

Only invisible assets can be simultaneously used in different places. A firm cannot have its workers in two different places at the same time, nor can the same floor space be simultaneously used for different purposes or the one piece of equipment produce simutaneously different products.

This simultaneous use has its origin in that an invisible asset is information-based. A basic property of information is that it can be used by two different people at the same time without reducing its amount or its value to any one of those people involved. Furthermore, the same piece of information can have very different values for different people. Hence invisible assets are not easily bought on the market-place and as economists have long known, a market for information is very hard to build.

The fourth reason why they are the competitive edge is that the value and the amount of the invisible assets will increase over time as they are used. This is the contrary of many physical assets, which are depleted or depreciated over time as they are used. This characteristic again stems from the fact that they are based on information. New combinations of different pieces or kinds of information increase the amount and can exponentially increase the value of information. This is the essence of innovation, the combining of disparate pieces of information in a new and creative way.

Before moving to answer the next question - how can we accumulate invisible assets for the competitive edge of the firm? - I want to stress the role of people in the development and maintenance of the firm's invisible assets. People are important because much of the invisible assets of a firm are embodied in people. It is people who carry and exchange the information necessary for competitive success. In emphasising the primacy of the information resources and channels of the firm, I may appear to be relegating people to the background. It is in fact impossible to separate people from the invisible assets which they carry. Engineers store technical knowledge in their brains. Workers acquire skills and savvy on the job. These are examples of embodied information. People are important as resources not just as participants in the labour force but as accumulators and producers of invisible assets.

Some invisible assets are embodied in people who do not work for the firm. The brand name is held by customers not employees. Saying that a firm has developed good channels for up-to-date market information implies that people in the distribution channel right down to those who work at the sales counters of shops which sell the firm's products are contributing by capturing and transmitting the necessary information into the firm.

There are two routes for the accumulation of invisible assets. The first is what I would call the direct route. In following this route, a firm puts resources into building invisible assets for the simple or exclusive objective of having them. Resources are explicitly spent for that purpose. A good example is a brand name created by a TV commercial. You pour money into it simply to have an asset called 'brand name'.

There is a second and, I believe, much more important route: the operations route. This is the accumulation of invisible assets virtually as a by-product of daily business operations. For example, a brand name becomes a valuable asset created by word-of-mouth communication because the firm has been providing a quality product to the customers. The quality properties of the product were essential to competitive success and not provided to build up the brand name only. But through the process a brand name has been developed and a reputation associated with it. This affects subsequent business operations positively. A company that has clearly superior products will develop information resources both in technology and in the distribution channel.

This route is also a relatively inexpensive route. Since the business operation has to be carried out in any event and should be carried out in the right manner, then the invisible asset as a by-product is in a sense free of charge. Many corporate resources necessary as inputs to the business operation are used up in the operation. Other resources also flow out of the operation as output. They have a dual character, and this makes them very important when divising a strategy.

Money is such a resource. It is a necessary input but also comes out of business activity as cash flow and profit. It can be recycled with the profit from a past project used to fund a future project. This dynamic nature of money has long been recognised by analysts. The dual nature of invisible assets is recogsiied by relatively few. As one founder said of his company, 'Matsushita is a company that creates people'. In other words, people's capabilities are an important output of a business operation as well as an input. In the normal course of business the firm acquires information not previously available. The accumulated and revised stock becomes the basis for the next project. Much of this stock, and in particular the skills to apply it to the company's business activities, are embodied in people.

The reason why we can have this product spill-over from a business operation to an invisible asset is that human beings are the primary means of information processing. Whenever a human being does something, he observes something or is observed by someone else. Because the human being has observation, learning and information-processing capacities, doing something always involves these informational activities. Whilst he is engaged in selling, a salesman is directly observing the market. He can convey the information he gathers through his day-to-day business operation of selling to the product development people. They can then accumulate that information for future input to the improved version of the product or to a new product.

The operations route is made possible by these informational capacities of the people engaged in them and also by the fact that from first product design to marketing or after-sales service, each business operation has an associated flow of information. Those involved in product development, for example, combine technological knowledge with information about consumer demand to develop new products. They do more than combine these existing pieces of information. They may be actively engaged in importing technological information from outside the firm through licensing or contracting work in universities. They are also learning new things in their laboratories or from the production engineers in the factories. Information flow is everywhere in the product development process.

In practice of course information is gathered or communicated wherever decisions are made or human observation takes place.

The effects may have a negative as well as a positive impact. During the course of a call to a customer by a salesman, the customer may volunteer information on his preference or may ask whether the company has a related product or is going to introduce one. If the reply is that 'We don't have it (or there is no demand for it) and I don't think that we will ever make it', he immediately has a twofold informational effect. First, the customer will see the firm as unresponsive to customer demands, and second, he will be cutting off the channel for information about the customers' needs.

Nikon provides an example of the negative effect on the existing stock of an invisible asset, its brand name and reputation. Nikon's reputation lay in being a manufacturer of cameras for sophisticated, professional users. It decided in the late 1970s to broaden its product line and introduce a mass-produced SLR camera with many plastic parts for the less-sophisticated user. This was a faster growing segment of the market in which other Japanese manufacturers were successfully operating. The decision was not made easily. There was serious concern. What would the long-time user or admirer of the high-quality and performance Nikon F think when he saw the less-sophisticated EM? Would the Nikon mystique, carefully cultivated and reinforced through all its operations, lose by association with this new but unsophisticated market?

The result was negative, a deterioration in overall performance and competitive edge. No major penetration of this new market segment was gained, and Nikon's reputation in the professional market declined. The way was opened for entry by the mass-market producers. This experience illustrates the delicate nature of brand image and how it can haunt the corporate strategist.

Ignoring the production of invisible assets in business operations or undervaluing them as an output also leads a company astray. A strategy designed with only effective utilisation of assets as input in mind is often incompatible with efficient accumulation of invisible assets as an output. Similarly, a strategy which may look wasteful or greedy in terms of outcomes from current operations may be a very effective way of accumulating information-based assets for future use.

A narrow focus on finance is a common cause of strategic failure, since the effect on the accumulation of invisible assets has been ignored. Withdrawal from a business with rich technological potential because return on investment will take a long time, has characterised many firms. Large US firms withdrew from the semiconductor business to their later chagrin. Too much emphasis on effective utilisation of current resources such as finance frustrates the accumulation of those invisible assets from which large profits would be obtained in the future.

Enrichment of the stock of information and increase in the capacity of the channels are the result of deliberate strategies to exploit the observation, learning and information-processing activities and the different information flows associated with daily and long-term business operations. An example of a strategy associated with the daily business operations is that of quality circles. Their very success has perhaps led them to be too narrowly understood. They are a group activity of workers in which they suggest improvements in the production methods, the kinds of materials which they should use or the kinds of designs the designers should be producing to reduce costs or improve quality. This is the well-known side of quality circles. The real reason behind the success of this kind of activity is the belief that those human beings working on a shop floor are capable of observation, learning and communicating. They have themselves an accumulated stock of information. They know something. Why not use them by giving them back their eyes and brains?. This strategy opens the communication channels and increases the information flow within the firm, and thereby increases receptivity to environmental information.

The key for accumulation of invisible assets for the long-term growth of the company is in controlling the flow of information. There are several ways of doing this, and, using the kind of conceptual framework proposed in this chapter, many interesting propositions for corporate strategy become possible. Corporate strategy should, for example, be somewhat destabilising in the sense that the firm should do something a little more than it is capable of doing at this moment in time. Through the process of actually doing that business which the firm is not capable of doing very well now, it will accumulate further invisible assets. The very reason for going into some business could be that we are not very good at it.

This sounds very contradictory. I call it the over-extension strategy. Joseph Bauer of Harvard Business School summarised this kind of strategy very well, when he said that 'this is like Robert Browning's adage. He said that a man's reach should exceed his grasp'. It can be a very beneficial strategy and one which Japanese firms have used very successfully. Firms in developing countries need to have this kind of over-extension strategy.

In seeking to control information flows, one must first identify what are the critical activities which will generate and communicate the most important information. One must then decide the means of control. For example, if the on-going trend of customer demand is identified as important information, then there are three options by which this information might be captured: selling directly to retailers and maintaining close contact with them, providing a sympathetic and responsive claims or after-sales service, or having daily contacts with customers by expanding into retailing. The decision must be based on evaluation of what mechanism will ensure that informaion actually flows as intended, both in quality and speed.

Internalising a critical activity is normally the best way to ensure initial proprietary access to information. Hence, some firms such as Hilti prefer direct distribution systems. Internalisation is also the control mechanism for development of technological skills. Many firms manufacture key components internally such as IBM with its memory chips. This is partly because of a wish to restrict sensititive information on key components, but it is also because the technological skill which they acquire will help them to develop a competitive final product. Internalisation is not always the best decision even if it looks good from an information control perspective. Some activities may require too much fixed investment to internalise. Partial internalisation, say 25 per cent of components made internally together with good mechanisms for control of information flow with suppliers of the rest, may be sufficient to retain competitive advantage.

Conclusion

Emphasising the importance of invisible assets and the informational aspect of a firm entails taking a certain kind of view of a firm and of what its core activities are. Economists tend to think of the firm as a collection of physical resources technologically transforming physical input into other kinds of physical output or services. Accountants tend to think about the firm as a sort of monetary transformation mechanism in which a certain amount of money will be increased to a greater amount of money and recorded in the accounting books.

Hence I have emphasised the view that the firm receives, accumulates and transmits information both with the environment and within the firm itself. The firm is a collection of human beings exchanging information with markets, with nature, among themselves, and processing and storing it. Only through this information processing and exchange can invisible assets be accumulated. This is certainly the age of information technology. In the final analysis, however, it is the human information activities which give competitive edge, and control of the information flows to build invisible assets has been and will be the most important activity of corporate executives.

5. Competence and strategy

Yves Doz

Professor of Business Policy
INSEAD, Fontainebleau, Paris

The central argument of this paper is that we need to view strategy as developing, using and exploiting core competences by applying them across a wide spectrum of different business opportunities. This is contrary to the concept of decentralised diversified multi-divisional companies typified by many European companies. In almost any European country we find industrial groups which are present in several different businesses and have many different product lines, but are small size in any of these product lines, as compared with global competitors in any individual business. Smaller diversified European companies can succeed only by over-coming such fragmentation.

As a starting-point let us look at the conventional strategic planning techniques and views which have been put forward by management consultants and a number of people doing research in business schools. We find that they put a lot of emphasis on product market strategies, on competing in individual product lines, on market positioning, on looking at the business units of the firm as separate units, and essentially making key decisions (such as, for instance, make or buy decisions), from the perspective of individual business units almost as if the rest of the company did not exist. A lot of focus has been put on the individual business units. While that kind of focus was useful in providing discipline at the business-unit managment level, a number of companies - for instance electronics groups in various European countries, such as GEC in the UK for a long time, and currently Thomson in France - by greatly decentralising their operations, may have been short-changing themselves.

They may have lost sight of the need to develop, nurture, deploy and leverage core competences in related businesses. Managers have not systematically asked questions such as, 'How do we think about core competences? How do we think about the ways in which those core competences are being cultivated, are being nurtured? How do we maintain the integrity of these competences?' And also, maybe, they have not taken the following view: 'We don't just compete on the product market-place, we may also be competing on the competence market-place in terms, for instance, of how do we attract the best software developers in an environment where the number of well-trained people is quite limited'.

The argument which comes increasingly to light as we study the less successful and the more successful European firms is that the companies which have taken too much of a decentralised product market view of business-unit management may be the ones which have been less successful over the long run. It is an approach which may be quite useful in the short run, to achieve a turnaround, but less useful in the long-run development of those companies.

We need to think of the firm in a way which is consistent with the argument presented by Professor Itami about the development of invisible assets. We should argue that the firm is really a portfolio of core competences which are deployed toward business opportunities, through organisational capabilities, in the sense of having the organisation capable of moving and applying those competences into multiple product market opportunities. To make the argument a little bit more concrete, we can consider two examples, one that of a well-known Japanese company and the other one that of a well-known European company.

Let me start with a very simplistic and simplified view of Honda, a company where one can argue that there is a very clear core competence which has been cultivated over a number of years, in the design, development and manufacture of gasoline engines.

The development of Honda over time has been accomplished by exploiting a series of new business opportunities, all of which drew on that core competence. Honda moved from motorcycles to automobiles, to lawnmowers, to chain saws, to generators, and so on. The characteristic common to all these products is that they are built around gasoline engines. That has allowed Honda to cultivate over the long run gasoline-engine technologies as a source of competitive advantage in each of those various businesses.

To take a European example, one can consider the Bic pen company and look at the evolution of Bic as parallel to that of Honda and many other successful companies. Bic started with two key competences - one in the shaping and fitting of plastics and metals very cheaply, but with a high quality and a high level of manufacturing precision, the other in mass distribution and advertising, distributing products through all kinds of drug stores, tobacco stores, mass merchandisers, and doing this very widely.

The Bic story, starting with pens, moving into lighters, into razors and so on, has been a story of leveraging and cultivating a very small number of core competences in a number of different application areas. Bic has been less successful in areas where they were straying far away from their basic manufacturing core competence such as panty hose. The current launch of discount perfumes capitalises on similar marketing competences and on some of the same manufacturing skills (e.g. plastic moulding).

This concept of strategic thinking is simply a matter of asking, 'How do we develop the company around a few core competences in ways that maximise the opportunities for the firm in multiple markets?' Now if one says, 'How do we develop a core competence? or How do we even think of our firm in terms of core competence?, I think that there are three critical questions the answers to which determine whether we have a useful core competence of great value or not. They are:

1. What significance does it have as a source of competitive differentiation? In other words, what kind of competitive advantage is it going to bring us vis-à-vis some of our competitors?
2. What is the potential breadth of applications? Is it a generic competence that can be used in multiple products lines in a reasonably similar way?
3. How durable is it in terms of a competitive differentiation? Or in other words, how difficult is it for competitors to imitate?

In this sense, what may be important to think through is that core competences are not just technology, they go beyond technology. Some of the competences that are likely to provide for long-term competitive differentiation of a sustainable nature against competition have a set of characteristics which make them system-embodied rather than stand-alone pieces of technology or machinery. They are tacit know-how capabilities rather than being explicitly technological. They are aggregative in nature, rather than merely innovative, that is they bring skills together rather than merely rely on innovations. They tend to be a concept of how to be excellent in some particular generic technology, so it is more than just one or another technology, it is a cluster of system technologies.

These can be very simple things. If I refer back to Bic, a good part of the success of Bic is simply based on this ability to manufacture precision small metal parts very cheaply, very effectively, with very high-quality standards, and to combine these with injection molded plastic parts, equally of precision quality. These are very simple technologies, but Bic does them in a way that offers better quality at a lower cost than most competitors. A core technical competence is built by blending a series of technologies rather than creating stand-alone technologies. A core competence is more an experience-based, tacit know-how which is acquired, developed and improved over a period of time rather than explicit knowledge. It is something which is deeply embodied in the organisation rather than something which is dependent on a couple of key scientists or a couple of marketing gurus. It is something which is difficult to transfer and difficult to acquire, and it is something which can be constantly improved upon which has to be constantly cultivated. The key concept is continuous improvement rather than one off revolutionary innovation. Hence it is not so much the ability of the firm to invent, as the ability to bring core competences together into a very focused development.

The issues involved in developing core competences tend to cluster around two questions: 'How do we learn and develop them?' and 'How do we leverage them to put them to the best possible use in multiple environments, both to serve the development of new businesses and to exploit existing businesses on an international scale?' The first question is partly answered - by improving the effectiveness of R & D. In European industry in general, providing more technology is not really the problem faced by most firms. It is not that firms are not scientifically or technologically competent. Overall, basic science or technology is not deeply deficient in Europe, when compared to the USA or Japan, nor is the problem for companies one of having access to basic science or basic technology, even if they don't develop these themselves. Furthermore, a number of new programmes like Esprit in the EEC, and a number of other efforts, have facilitated the development, acquisition and exchange of basic scientific knowledge.

The issue is much more one of effectiveness of R & D management in the sense of translating that scientific knowledge into usable new products, systems and services. The other problem in many European companies, in the electronics industry in particular, is essentially a problem of the timescale of the market for new products. The profitability of market opportunities in a number of industries is affected by shorter product life-cycles, with most of the profits being made early in the life-cycle of a new product. This calls for much more speedy, much more effective, much more timely new product development. That is really where a number of businesses in Europe tend to run into trouble. They ultimately come up with the products, but late, when the new businesses are no longer very profitable, and when they cannot always recover their initial R & D costs.

The first item on the competitiveness agenda of a number of European companies in terms of developing core competences is this question of effectively using available scientific knowledge and translating it into new product development in a timely enough fashion. They need to address all kinds of issues around the management of product development: the use of product development teams, the evolution of those teams over time, the transition from research into development, the interface between development and marketing, and the ability to create more entrepreneurship.

The second issue, in my view, is being very sensitive to core skills. This goes back to looking at the company not as a set of discrete product business units, as if the rest of the company did not exist, but rather to thinking of the company as a bundle of skills and to saying, 'How are the various decisions that we take in terms of research, in terms of new product development, in terms of marketing and distribution channels, advertising and reputation vis-à-vis customers, and so on, affecting the core skills of the company?' In summary this involves making product market choices from the standpoint of core competences, and ensuring that such choices contribute to the nurturing of core competences.

The third issue, and one which is an interesting opportunity for companies, is the use of partnerships. In other words, how to use partnerships for collaborative research, for joint manufacturing with others, and for market access not just as a way to gain economies of scale or as a way to decrease the cost of doing research or to make it more affordable and so on, but also as a way to learn new skills. Very explicit attention has to be paid to 'How do we learn from other companies new skills that we cannot afford to develop on our own but which exist already?'.

There are some very interesting European examples. For instance, Thomson in France have a joint venture in the VCR (video cassette recorders) business with JVC, the Japanese innovator in that field which introduced the VHS format. Through that joint venture Thomson has learnt from their Japanese partner a number of new manufacturing technologies as well as enough product technology to put them in a position to develop and manufacture competently, on their own, should they wish, up-to-date VCRs. If you look back five years, Thomson had missed the VCR boat, whereas now they have acquired the option to pursue VCR technology alone. Companies should be saying, 'How do we use partnerships to make up for delays, for missed opportunities, or for skill deficiencies?' Another European company, Olivetti, has used fairly successfully a number of different partnerships to learn new skills and complement its own portfolio of technologies quite usefully at a low cost. Skill-based partnerships, with explicit attention paid to maximising learning, can thus be used as a means to acquire, rather than develop, core competences.

The fourth priority is to screen new business opportunities based on core skills. For managers it is to say, 'Let's think about new businesses not as unrelated diversification but more as related diversification efforts which need either to exploit the existing core skills, to draw on them for further business development or to create the opportunity to bring into the company new core skills which are going to complement those we already have'. The result may be either easier organic new business development or very well targeted technology acquisitions which are going to complement the portfolio of skills and capabilities.

The fifth priority is an obvious one: European companies need to leverage their businesses internationally better than they have done so far. Essentially they need to think about how to develop their businesses on a global scale rather than just how to compete in domestic markets. This is a major problem in many technology-intensive industries in nearly all European countries

Yet, having the competences, and even more having a portfolio of mutually reinforcing competences, is not sufficient - that is only one side of the equation - companies also need to be able to mobilise within the organisation and apply these competences to all the new opportunities which are identified. This brings into perspective the other side of the equation of corporate strategy, the requirement to have a set of organisational capabilities with which to make competences and opportunities.

The first, step is to give enough visibility to the performance of the individual business unit. European companies have been good at this and we should not abandon the process. However, in conjunction with this companies should bring more effort to bear on intensifying the capability for inter-unit communication and collaboration. This must obviously be based on managing the information flow within the firm in order to create enough shared information and enough exchange of information between these business units. Beyond information it requires incentives for business unit managers to collaborate one with the other, rather than to ignore each other or to compete against each other within the company. This in turn leads to the need to shift the nature of inter-division relationships within large companies from one where there is perception of zero sum gain in transactions between divisions. It is not a question of one division getting the money and another not, a view based on the concept of physical assets referred to by Professor Itami. It is a question of perceiving that by collaborating, each division ends up being better off in the long term.

Internal culture then shifts in our companies from one of competition to one of selective collaboration, a vision of division managers being much more able to say, 'Let's collaborate selectively on some issues when it is of mutual benefit to all of us.'

Differentiation and interdependence in managing innovation is seemingly a paradox. One needs to create enough difference, enough autonomy for new businesses to be developed, and at the same time enough interdependence for the core skills to be exploited. The example of the IBM personal computer development is a very interesting one from that standpoint. It was developed by being able to draw on the resources and invisible assets of IBM, but at the same time in a very entrepreneurial mode, far away, not only geographically but also in internal culture, from the heaviness and the thoroughness of corporate headquarters. The management of the PC division had a lot of autonomy to develop itself and to borrow its management practices and style from companies like Apple rather than having to copy the management styles of the system businesses of IBM. On the one side, we want to be flexible in differentiating the way in which various new businesses and new products are being managed, and yet on the other be able to have new businesses and products draw on some of the core competences of the company.

A further point concerns the way in which corporate management, essentially the top management, helps the business units to manage the core competences. The critical function of information flow mangement is to make sure that the messages being sent to the division managers or to the business unit managers are not inconsistent with the development of core competences. If the view is constantly one of saying, 'What matters is short-term profit over the next three months', you end up effectively with asset stripping, getting money out of the company without regard to long-term effects. You cannot provide or you do not provide the amount of slack and the amount of encouragement for business-unit managers to develop under their own steam or to be willing to develop on their own inter-unit communication and collaboration.

Finally there is the issue with which a number of companies are struggling. This is how to manage projects and give resources to projects which cut across multiple units and where these projects are actually developing or encouraging the development of core competences within the company but are not particularly attractive to individual companies. They may, for example be R & D budgets and projects or projects to develop manufacturing skills.

To summarise the arguments, the critical proposition is that European companies, particularly technology-intensive ones, start from a position of disadvantage, where they have initially diversified rather broadly as multi-divisional companies and in the context of one single country. In order to compete against some of the global competitors, they need to make sure that the various businesses build upon each other, contribute to the development of core competences and use these core competences to build their competitive advantage. This is the route followed by successful companies. The model of managing much more along core competence lines than along autonomous business-unit lines, demands much more intensive information flows within the organisation. It really takes us back to this question of managing information and of organising to do this. The critical success factor for matching opportunities and core competences is one of having widely shared information within the firm. This is very contrary to our traditional view of trying to segment and fragment the information and trying to keep it at the business specific level or trying to keep it at the corporate level. It assumes a much freer flow of information and a much richer flow of information within the company, both between businesses and between corporate management and business-unit management. It assumes also a freer flow of information if we want to leverage businesses and innovations internationally, a freer flow of information between the country of origin of the company and its international operations. Management must devote attention to different ways of facilitating the flow of information and removing the barriers to the flow.

One approach is to create the incentive for the business unit managers to collaborate with each other, essentially to move away from a scheme of measurement and rewards in the company which is based purely on a business-unit-performance level to one which is blended much more with group performance, the role in helping the development of core technologies, and so on.

Another is to create a way of allocating resources not specifically to individual businesses or individual functions, but to programmes that cut across functions and businesses in such a way as to build more competences for the firm. A third dimension is for management to encourage that kind of behaviour. This assumes that top management is much more directly involved in managing the substance of the business, is not just taking a banker's role, is not just looking at each of the individual business units as a piece of a portfolio investment, but is taking a very active role in thinking through this question of, 'What are the most relevant core technologies and how can we best leverage them?'

To compete on the basis of core competences requires a number of changes. It is not just a question of providing more information. The issue is not one of saying, 'We ought to use information technology better' or 'We used to do environmental scanning better', and so on. That is not enough. The real question is to encourage and to make feasible more horizontal collaboration by working with managers within individual business units, through programmes which get resources across existing business units, and by having top management play a much more active role in managing the totality of the firm as a portfolio of core competences.

The transformation agenda a number of European companies have to go through, or are going through currently, consists of moving away from the sub-unit view to the core-competency view.

6. The impact of information and information technology on the structure of the firm

Bruno Lamborghini

Vice President

Corporate Strategic Analysis and Planning
Olivetti, Italy

Information is becoming the true strategic resource, the invisible asset of the manufacturing company. This concept raises a number of questions regarding the effective use, means of production, utilisation and diffusion of information by the firm on the one hand and on the other about the ever-increasing range of information technology equipment which is available today.

The increasing diffusion of information technologies in products, in production processes and in organisation is bringing about profound changes in the structures of firms and in their strategies. There is as yet no brake to the extraordinary development of the basic microelectronic components which are pushing dramatically the development of information technologies. The rate of growth in components during the next four to ten years will see

- processing power of microprocessors doubling every two and a half years;
- the capacity of Random Access Memory being quadrupled every three years;
- hard disk capacity doubling every two years.

Integration and globalisation

This rapid evolution in components is the basic factor of change, a phenomenon that is creating a rapid evolution and building up a pressure for many other changes. Information technologies modify traditional separations between technological areas and industrial sectors. New markets are being created and others modified.

Inside information technologies themselves there is increasing integration not only between components and hardware but between these and software, information management and information transportation. New kinds of services are growing up under the pressure of this rapid evolution of the technology.

The pressure to integrate is particularly challenging in the unification occurring in what were once two separate worlds, the world of telecommunications and the world of the office. The rapid growth in networks stems from the technological pressure and a firm's need to integrate telecommunications, data processing and office automation. Integration is occurring in other spheres which further impel technological evolution. The political and economic integration of Europe is forcing the unification of the European telecommunications networks, and this will have its further impacts on technologies, services, suppliers and consumer demands.

In this, Europe typifies what is happening in the larger global context. The world is becoming a global village. This means more than international markets. It means that we must think globally in terms of geographical markets. Managers and firms must think in terms of open business. Not only are markets becoming open but so also are technologies, industrial sectors, products and culture. Information technology itself is a major force in the push to globalisation, changing totally the scenario in which we work. Globalisation breaks frontiers, traditionally protected niches and oligopolistic environments. Everyone, large or small companies is obliged to think in terms of openness.

An era of discontinuity

The present era is an era of discontinuity at both a macroeconomic and microeconomic level. It is a time of macroeconomic change between two eras, the industrial one of the last 200 years and the new post-industrial era based on information technology and being driven by information technology as the steam and later engines drove the industrial era. It is a time when we must change completely the way we think.

As the most reactive organisation, the manufacturing firm is at the centre of this discontinuity. The forces created by information technology and globalisation are concentrated at this micro-level of the firm. Firms themselves in their reaction to information technology and its diffusion then become the major determinants of the speed and conditions of IT diffusion on and throughout the whole of society.

In adapting to these pressures and changes and to a world of openness, firms must develop flexibility in order to be open themselves. A company has to learn how to reach a real global integration. New complex forms of management are required of technologies, manufacturing, marketing and finance. It means moving from an export-oriented approach, manufacturing in one country and exporting to others or from the traditional multinational approach based on directly controlled structures abroad. To meet change and grasp the new opportunities, means developing a new kind of structure. This structure is more similar to a network of relationships between companies and virtually independent units in the various countries linked together through common strategic functions with co-ordinated management of human resources, finance, technology and with a consensus on objectives, values and corporate identify. This network of relations must, however, also be extended to external partners of the company, suppliers, distributors, technology and other partners and finally to customers, the market. The skilful management of innovative pressures coming from technology and globalisation becomes the formula for survival and success in this era of discontinuity.

In examining some of the features of the new types of organisation that are required, I want to start with two basics of a firm, the factory and the office. These have become the strategic areas of change. Traditionally, the factory has been and still is the central area of the company organisation where the major technological innovations have been introduced and where the major organisational efforts have been made. This has been the case since the beginning of the Industrial Revolution.

The office, and by office I mean all the non-manufacturing activities of the firm, has been mainly considered almost as an appendix, a secondary area of the company whose function was to support the manufacturing activities. Efforts to improve productivity have been concentrated on increasing that of manufacturing. Hence, mechanisation and then automation have been centred on the factory floor, replacing human energies and skills with mechanical ones and thereby multiplying labour productivity.

The factory

Factory automation is in fact as old as the Industrial Revolution. Today we talk of robotisation and FMS (flexible manufacturing systems) but these are only a phase of a long process which started with the introduction of the steam engine. They are being adopted within the framework of traditional thinking. Now we seem to be entering upon a new phase in this era of discontinuity. In this phase, under the pressures originating in the new technologies and globalisation, new forms of organisation are required at the factory level in order to change completely the traditional approaches.

The factory organisation lies at the centre of pressures which are both internal and external. Those from inside include rising costs and complexity. The ones from outside include the demands for quality, delivery, flexibility, shorter lead times and the greater competition. Quality is becoming the real leading edge of competitiveness for all companies and for all activities.

A flow of new opportunites with attractive names like CAD, CAM, FMS and Robots is being offered every day to the factory which has problems in meeting the external and internal pressures and demands. What is drastically changing is the kind of products requested by the market. Until now, the accent has been on standardisation and mass production. This has changed. The accent is more and more on diversification, diversified product ranges and diversified production, customisation, flexibility and quality.All levels of company, large and small, are moving from a Fordistic production system or factory to a flexible specialisation production system in order to make rapid changes in production, cope with shorter productlife-cycles, meet greater competition and meet the high-quality demands of the market. In fact we are moving from the concept of factory automation to the concept of the factory of the future.

Every day one can read this phrase in the newspapers, but the phrase, 'factory of the future' in reality is something different. It is not only a matter of words, it is a problem of meaning, of different objectives. It implies in a new and complex way the utilisation of all the opportunities offered by technology, techniques and organisational approaches. Amongst these latter are Just-in-Time, total quality control, design for manufacturing, group technology, and so on, and structural factors like vertical integration and functional integration.

This total and integrated utilisation of new technical and methodological opportunities has the objective of responding with new outputs like flexibility, continuity, consistency, quality, precision, and so on, to the new requests coming from a global market. The process of automation is moving from the pure automation of single activities, intra-activity automation, to integrated automation of the different activities in each area, intra-sphere automation, and finally to the integrated automation of all the activities of the various areas (inter-sphere automation).

The introduction of Flexible Manufacturing Systems, which can be defined as a series of manufacturing activities which are interlinked by means of a common control and transport system, permitting frequent variations of the operations, is an intermediary step towards the creation of the factory of the future, but it is not the factory of the future. The new forms of factory organisation no longer have the objective of simple factory automation where the 'unmanned factory' was the final step. A new approach like CIM, Computer Integrated Manufacturing, is designing new integrated manufacturing systems where the output is not only physical but also immaterial, the information flow and the capacity to interact in a creative way with the whole company organisation and also with the external environment. We must no longer talk of factory automation but of integrated and interactive manufacturing environments. CIM is a step forward towards the implementation of the factory of the future, but what is more important the factory of the future has to become the enterprise of the future through an integrated reorganisation with the other strategic area, the office and 'non-manufacturing' side of the company.

The office

As in the the factory, a revolution is also taking place in the office environment. In the past, the office, even if in a more limited way than the manufacturing area, saw investment in mechanisation processes with the objective of increasing labour productivity. Then, during the past ten years under the pressures of increased costs of office labour and decreasing productivity, office automation has become very popular. Office automation has had the same objective as factory automation, that is to replace human resources with mechanical resources. But the results were very poor compared to what happened at the factory level. Developments in technology are now leading to a switch in objectives. With the process of tertiarisation and information, the office is becoming the centre of the company, replacing the position held in the past by the factory.

New architectures have developed based on a co-operative approach where networks of PCs at work-group level are interconnected through LANs, with networks of minicomputers at departmental level and with mainframes at central level. A new interest has been taken in the office environment, and to create this environment new forms of organisation are required. Office automation is being replaced by a new concept: OIS (Office Integrated Systems), very similar in principle to CIM. The objective in the office, as in the factory, is no longer to mechanise or reduce human labour but to create an integrated flow of information with high added value. In fact, organisations are now beginning to 'think' of their offices as 'fully-integrated networks' where individuals, work-groups and corporate staff can work, exchange information and communicate voice, text, data and images, both internally and externally.

Today's transition from the traditional office automation approach to the office integrated system is therefore driven by:

- the ability of individual workers to create, access, manipulate and communicate information;
- the search for a corporate-wide approach to establish an architectural framework and to plan a support system for any combination of information - data, text, image-graphic or voice;
- the increasing effectiveness of managers and professionals in the OIS environment.

OIS is characterised by three major characteristics:

- integration;
- connectivity;
- communication.

Integration is the first concern of organisations involved in OIS projects. The large installed base existing now in organisations represents an investment that must be preserved. In fact, the office environment today is a mix of technologies and products where totally different kinds of equipment are installed without reciprocal links (telephone, typewriters, PCs, terminals, teleprinters, copiers, file systems, etc.). They do not talk to each other. The problem is to try to integrate and permit communication between the different equipment used in the office and between the old and the new.

As a result, standards and compatibility requirements are now emerging. You read every day of open system interconnection, of open software foundation, and of new operating systems which have the possibility of permitting connection between equipment of different manufacturers. It is a trend of such a momentum that even companies with proprietary systems such as IBM are entering into this new phase of open standards.

Connectivity is the second key-factor in OIS. Mainframes, departmental systems, servers, PCs, other office workstations and peripherals have to be able to talk together to optimise the information system and to make the overall corporate information system efficient and flexible.

The third factor is clearly communication. The transfer of information is the basic objective of office work; there can be no office system without a flow of information. You have to create the real flow of communications within the company and outside your company with your partners, suppliers and customers. In an organisation, 10 per cent of created information is distributed outside the establishment while 90 per cent circulates within the building. As a result, both wide area and local area communications are strategic in every organisation.

Naturally, with the improvement of electronic communication capabilities within the organisation it is necessary to face the security problems that emerge from the increasing level of 'system distribution'. Centralisation means a control of 'flows' while distributed architectures lead to autonomy and information access. The distribution of data among many departmental computers makes it far more difficult to track, manage and protect sensitive information.

Another problem is cost justification, which in some cases has a misleading approach due to the difficulties that exist in measuring office productivity and putting a value on information generated or communicated. Furthermore, negative experience in office automation has shown that other factors determine uncalculated costs:

- worker training;
- 'cultural' acceptance of innovation.

Training often diminishes the short-term productivity of the office and, in many cases, must not be considered as a one time variable. In fact, given that technology acceleration shortens product lifecycles, the learning curve often represents a significant part of the product use period.

A 'cultural' refusal can often have a dramatic economic effect on investment.

An integrated network

With the new forms of organisation required by technology and globalisation, the two traditionally separated environments, the factory and the office, are trying to grow in terms of integration, to converge on each other and to create a real information flow within their own organisation and structure. CIM and OIS can represent a path towards the integration of physical and information flows at company level, but we are still far from the possibility of a real convergence of the two areas.

Changes in organisation, to be effective, have to be developed in an integrated network which includes all areas of the company structures and where information can flow throughout the whole organisation. Thus, to manage physical and logical flows through a really integrated information system becomes the key factor in achieving high quality, cost reduction and better competitive performance. In other words, we need to converge the two areas in order to reach a real integrated network at company level.

Otherwise we will not use information in an effective way and in the best way. Nor will we use the potential of the equipment and the technology even as available today.

Communication becomes a vital element of the organisation. Companies tend to become networks of information, products and decisional flows. Networks are developed inside and outside the companies. New forms of networks are developed with other companies, suppliers and customers. The Japanese have actively promoted this approach and developed a very synergistic network between users and manufacturers. This approach presents fundamental advantages in its being a flexible and adaptive system and in reducing the costs of adaptation to change. Above all, it has a built-in innovative multiplier, many innovations come from the chain of suppliers and customers. This is an aspect that we in Europe have not yet achieved. The network has to be developed not only with the natural partners of a company, suppliers on one side and users and customers on the other, but also with the territory, the geographical area where the company is located. The more global a company becomes, the more necessary becomes the creation of a strong integration and interdependence with the territory where the company is located. In today's conditions only a real synergistic relationship between a company and its territory can provide an innovative and challenging support to the development of the competitiveness of a company.

The transition to this new phase is not easy and encounters obstacles of which the major ones are conservatism and a scarce propensity to make the 'quantum jump' in attempting to integrate different cultures within a firm. Huge investments in automation give only a limited answer to new requirements. Gradualism and fragmentation tend to limit the possibility of a real jump in organisation. It becomes evident that improvements through partial optimisation processes like in the factory at factory level are not sufficient and tend to increase cost or to cause failures.

New technologies applied to an organisation whose culture remains based on a 'Fordistic' philosophy can have negative effects. Evident failures in applying a revolutionary change in organisation at manufacturing level or in the office while not changing the culture of people are clear indications that today the most critical factor is culture change. The development of new forms of organisation integrating and networking the different areas inside and outside the company and the possibility to use new kinds of information technology products and equipment are less and less limited by technological factors. They are limited by 'human' factors. The solution is to train people who can understand and implement what is requested in a phase of radical discontinuity and actively participate in this phase of change and in the development of networks.

The experience of Olivetti is the response of an information-technology (IT) player to a changing industry scenario under the pressures coming from information technologies, from the growing role of information, from market globalisation and from new organisational requirements. The IT sector is in some sense anticipating what is going to happen in all of industry. The response given by Olivetti is to become a real global corporation through the development of a complex multidimensional organisation, the extension of an international network of alliances and partnerships, the integration of manufacturing and the coordination of distribution channels, having defined clearly the strategic objectives and established the control of the three main resources, human, finance and technology. The management of human resources is in fact becoming the key strategic issue.

Creation of a network of independent units with autonomous responsibility and strategy can create confusion. It becomes difficult to reach the real objectives of the company and it becomes more like a traditional conglomerate. The answer is the definition of strategic objectives and control of the three main resources from the centre. Otherwise, the network can quickly be transformed into a very confused environment.

Starting from the classical model of a centralised mutinational based on direct structures abroad, Olivetti has transformed itself into an articulated and complex network of independent companies strongly linked together through common objectives, the sharing of common resources and a clearly defined co-ordination system. Within this network, it is important that each company and even each segment or division of the company should think and act like an autonomous company, a profit centre with a clear responsibility and having specific missions and strong roots in its local market. I must underline this last point. Even a very large and very global company, one which has reached the kind of globalisation required by the present scenario, must be strongly rooted in its different local markets.

The management of such a network requires the right direction and the avoidance of competition inside. One of the most difficult things to do if you create a competitive environment within your company and your group is to ensure that this competition does not kill the company. Technology management has also become much more complex. The extraordinary role of innovation in IT shortens dramatically product life-cycles, widens the technology arena and raises R & D and engineering costs. It becomes impossible for an IT company, even if the largest one, to respond to the technological challenge only through internal resources. What is required is the development of a network of agreements, alliances, partnerships and new kinds of dynamic interdependences and synergies at world-wide level.

Olivetti strategy is based on the consideration that competition is today no longer just between individual companies, even large companies like IBM but between mobile and expanding networks of companies, related together, even competitors, according to a world-wide logic which overrides their own national identities. They are expanding networks, but they can change day by day. You have to be flexible to understand what is happening. The synergies in the network have to be optimised otherwise the network can create a very negative effect.

The 1992 deadline of the unification of the European market will accelerate this tendency to creation of networks of companies. At the same time the 1992 deadline of an open market will be accelerated by the reaction of European companies themselves in facing up to this challenging date. Since the end of the 1970s Olivetti has closely followed and developed this strategy of creating a network of alliances with partners of small and large size, from the more than forty venture-capital investments into small high-tech firms to the partnerships with large companies such as AT & T, Toshiba, Bull and so on.

At the same time, the network model has been developed inside the company through the transformation of internal departments into independent companies or independent business units, the acquisition of new companies, the start-up of new initiatives, the creation of joint ventures even with competitors, and the participation in co-operative research activities. ESPRIT, the European initiative in information technology and other European programmes are very much helping to generate interaction between European companies. They develop a common base of understanding and thus prepare the way for this kind of new model of organisation.

Today, more than 200 independent firms, from the very small ones to the large ones coexist and positively co-operate within the Olivetti Group.

The success of managing this complex system of networks inside and outside the company with partners representing a variety of cultures, strategies and organisation is strictly dependent on the capacity to create an effective network of information based on formal and informal procedures. The effectiveness of information networks is reachable through the development of a truly open information system and a very balanced information flow, but the crucial point is the level of culture, responsibility and participation of people within the network. It requires investment to promote a dynamic process of organisation change through the use of technology, best information and through permanent training. The best use of technology occurs when it is targeted to the best development of the human resources which are today the most strategic assets of a company.

7. Technical change and competitiveness

E. Sciberras

Director, Regional Industrial Research Unit
University of Newcastle upon Tyne

The aim of this chapter is to contribute to understanding the forces which shape information flows, organisation change and structural adjustment by firms who have been successful in adopting technical change. My thesis is that to understand information and organisational change one must first understand the nature of the major points of impact of technical change in the firm itself and then from there understand what role information and organisational change plays and where they fit in. It is based on research conducted over a number of years into a diverse range of industries both internationally and in the north of England and involving some 200 firms.

For successful firms, technical change has affected and requires adjustment firstly to the firm's goals, planning and decision-making, and then to its products, marketing and investment policies. It also requires change to the structure of the organisation, the degree and extent of vertical and horizontal integration, as well as changes to its manpower both in terms of the skill profile and how and where they are deployed.

Reference is made to each of these to see how information flow and structural change and adjustment have been necessitated by technical change.

A microeconomic approach

Many institutions in society are involved in the development and generation of technical change. They include universities, research establishments and firms. The nature of these institutions' relationship and involvement with technical change depends upon their objectives. Universities are often concerned with new technology for the generation of knowledge and understanding in its own right. Other research establishments may be concerned with the more applied aspects of technical change to solve problems which interest them or their clients and sponsors.

The relationship of firms with technical change is different. In some important respects the relationship of firms to technical change may be the most important of all. Although other institutions also develop and generate new knowledge and solve problems, it is only when firms adopt technical change and 'run with it' that new technology begins to have a widespread impact on society, the workforce and on international competitiveness in particular. In order to understand the pattern of diffusion of technical change and its impact, it is first necessary therefore to understand the motivations and strategies of firms and why they adopt technical change.

Firms are not interested in new technology for its own sake. To draw an analogy with combat, firms are involved in a constant competitive battle of greater or lesser intensity depending on the technical maturity and extent of industrial concentration in an industry. The ultimate indicators of success over rivals in this battle and therefore the goals of the firm, are long-run profitability and market share. To fight, firms use the 'weapons' of products (their features, quality and price), investment, manufacturing and manpower, and sometimes they enlist government protection and support.

Firms' interest in technical change is in the way in which it can contribute to their ability to fight or compete. Technology is not a weapon in itself. It is a means of sharpening and increasing the impact of weapons. The deployment and use of these weapons and the means by which technical change opportunities are exploited are determined in the battle plan or competitive strategy of the firms. The central underlying hypothesis of this research therefore is that in order to understand the relationship of technical change to competiveness it is necessary to understand the competitive behaviour of firms in industry. This brings the analysis firmly into the province of the microeconomic theory of the firm.

The goals of the firm, product differentiation, investment and production have been accepted as major subjects of analysis of firms' behaviour in microeconomic theory for a long time. However, their treatment under neoclassical marginal analysis, while theoretically elegant, is too static and unrelated to the real world to be of use to industrialists and policy-makers. (For a review and critique by the author of some major contributions in the theory of the firm, see Sciberras 1977, chs. 1 and 2, and Sciberras, Senkar and Swords-Isherwood 1977.)

Goals and planning

The goals firms pursue are not simply dictated by the structure of the market (although they are influenced by it). Nor, for successful firms, are they simply dictated by immediate commercial pressures or the conditions of the current phase of the product cycle. Successful firms act upon the world - not merely react to it. They choose their goals strategically in the interests of long-term competitiveness.

The goals adopted by firms can significantly affect their ability or willingness to adopt new technology. For example, in some sectors of industry, increased standardisation in new products enabling lower costs and increased reliability, has become an important factor in success. In order to obtain the long-term competitive benefits of standardisation, firms in such sectors have to be prepared to resist pressures to customise. Firms which adopt short-run goals to survive or defend market share are more likely to reject the longer-term benefits of standardisation and accept a significant degree of customer-specified engineering in their products.

Developments in manufacturing process, involving more extensive automation, enable substantial competitive advantages. Such equipment is expensive, however, and requires a long payback on investment compared with conventional equipment. Firms which adopt short-run profit goals are more likely to assess advanced manufacturing equipment as unprofitable and resort to investment in conventional machines with a quick payback. Firms which adopt long-run goals are more likely to accept the higher short term costs of such equipment and obtain the longer-term competitive benefits over their rivals.

The achievement of long-term goals does not result from firms simply indentifying and placing themselves on intersections of some predetermined cost and revenue curves. Planning establishes the means that firms will adopt to achieve their goals. The requirement for, and effectiveness of, planning are important factors in firms' ability to adopt technical change for competitive success. It includes firms' financial arrangements and budgeting as well as product, manufacturing and investment planning. The nature of and requirement for planning and its relationship to competitive success may, however, be different for different industrial segments.

Firms need to understand the needs of a diverse and large number of users. These needs have to be translated into an appropriate range of products to cover the targeted user segment. Getting this wrong means introducing products that users do not want. Competitive success requires planning the right product range at the right price. To achieve low cost, firms try to maximise component standardisation in their products. This requires effective planning of product design. Failure to do this loses the significant cost advantages available.

An important aspect of competitive success in major product segments is maximising production volume. Firms must estimate and accurately determine required volumes. This needs the planning of the likely levels of demand ahead of the market.

Firms also need to plan volume production. This requires ordering components and scheduling production well into the future. Firms also need to determine the most appropriate manufacturing techniques. This includes planning manufacturing equipment, factory layout and the sequence of production. Advanced manufacturing equipment requires a careful assessment of return on investment because of its high purchase cost. Effective production planning is necessary to achieve maximum utilisation of expensive capital equipment.

With rapidly changing technology, firms must also plan to ensure that future needs for, perhaps, an entirely different mix of skills, often in technologies far removed from their traditional experience, will be available as their demands change. Firms also need to determine the appropriate mix of skills that will be needed in senior management to make long-term decisions about investments in new and rapidly changing product and manufacturing technologies.

Effective planning may require close collaboration of management in all areas of the firm including product engineering and manufacturing as well as marketing and financial management. This willingness of firms to accept a balanced contribution from all these functions may be an important factor in the adoption of technical change for competitive success.

Product policy

Product policy includes policies for product standardisation or differentiation, marketing and the organisation of managerial responsibility and for decision-making about products. The type of product segments in which the firm competes affects the product policies adopted. Generally, different strategies are necessary for competitive success in the different segments. Successful product policy involves important strategic considerations not adequately described by Chamberlin's or Bain's notions of product differentiation. Nor is it dependent solely on exploitation of innovation leads through clever pricing strategies of the Sylos-Labini type.

Meeting market needs and appropriate pricing are critical to success, but these are only part of policy consideration for successful firms. Abernathy and Utterback (1975) identified some of the interdependencies such as standardisation, but saw this as evidence of innovative decline and omitted some major ones such as the need for managerial realignment in product policy decision-making.

Standardisation in product design to reduce the number and variety of components is important for competitiveness. It reduces costs for firms by minimising the stocks of components they need to hold and may yield economies of bulk component purchases. Standardisation also reduces costs by reducing the variety and amount of assembly necessary in production. The lower the variety of parts, the higher is the reliability of the final product. The fewer the breakdowns, together with easier maintenance and the smaller number and variety of spares needed to be held in stock, the lower is the cost of after-sales service. Increased product standardisation is the result of technical change and itself enables more technical change in production. Technical change in electronics has significantly reduced the number of parts in the many products of industries such as telecommunications equipment, machine tools, office equipment, watches and other consumer durables. The reduction in the variety of parts itself reduces costs, but the resulting potential for greater throughput of similar parts makes more feasible the adoption of automation in manufacturing process. This can further reduce costs and increase precision and reliability in a 'virtuous circle' of competitive benefits.

Although new technology has created the opportunities for standardisation, the realisation of these benefits requires firms to be able and willing to design and develop products around a narrower range of components. Firms may be aware of the benefits of standardisation and may attempt to design and develop products to obtain these benefits, but there may be a significant difference between firms in their willingness to insist on retaining design control over their products and to standardise. The degree of acceptance often depends on the relative influence within the firm of product engineers, marketing management and manufacturing engineers. The appropriate balance between these three functions may vary between industrial segments.

In major product segments firms need to acquire the type of balance that involves marketing in identifying broad market needs and translating these so that the firm's product engineers can design a general, standard product line that is both acceptable to the market and able to obtain the benefits of standardisation. Aggressive marketing firms go out with the advantages of low prices and high reliability that standardisation has made possible, and persuade users to accept the firms' standard product. The involvement of manufacturing engineering in product design to secure the ability to apply advanced manufacturing techniques and to operate the efficient production layout and schedule, ensures that the features attractive to the market and the features desired by the product engineers still add up to a makeable and cost competitive product.

Firms which achieve the appropriate balance of all three functions are more likely to develop and introduce the product technology that the market wants and to manufacture these products in the most cost-effective way to achieve competitive success.

Research, design and development

It is often difficult to obtain an accurate impression of the extent, nature and deployment of technical effort by firms in industry. Research, design and development expenditures, or numbers of employees engaged full time in formal R & D give a very imprecise indication of firms' total technical effort.

R & D indicators do not distinguish between those firms which do significant amounts of basic research and those firms which do little basic research but concentrate large resources in formal design and development efforts. In the case of the latter, particular divisions of vertically integrated firms which do little basic research themselves, may benefit from basic research done elsewhere in the organisation such as in central laboratories or in other technically advanced divisions. These research activities are not reflected in the R & D efforts of the particular division itself but may make a very important contribution to its technical capabilities and performance.

The distribution of research and development effort between parents' central laboratories and a particular division's own laboratories, and within firms, between their product development and manufacturing engineering activities, can be an important factor in understanding the competitiveness of firms and the nature of their technical strength in competition.

Another important contributor to firms' technical efforts are developments which take place outside of the formal R & D facilities of the parent or the firm. These 'informal' efforts include product design modifications or improvements and applications software developments which enhance the 'user friendliness' of products or offer variations in functions. These are usually undertaken by product engineering departments. Informal efforts also include improvements in design for manufacturability undertaken in consultation with manufacturing engineers, or improvements in the layout and organisation of production which result from learning and experience gained in manufacturing.

These informal efforts are sometimes estimated to account for a larger share of total technical expenditure and manpower than formal R & D and to contribute very significantly to a firm's competitive performance. Not only are the absolute levels of these informal efforts important. As with formal R & D, the distribution of the informal technical effort between product engineering and manufacturing activities in the firms influence their performance and reflect their strategic emphasis in competition.

Investment and manufacturing

Investment and manufacturing policy determines the types of equipment purchased by firms and the features that firms seek in the new equipment they purchase. The neoclassical representation of firms' investment strategy is one of a confrontation by the firm of a series of externally-given production possibilities. These are embodied in imaginary isoquant curves, (expressed in hardware terms as alternative production technology or machinery and labour combinations) between which the firm must choose.

This entirely misrepresents the firm and the competitive process in the real world. The actual capital-to-labour ratio realised in production is as much a function of a firm's manufacturing management objectives and efficiency as it is an attribute of the machine or production technique. Further, as Sylos-Labini, Abernathy and others have demonstrated, successful firms seek more than short-run efficiency in deciding upon the timing, nature and level of production technology in which they will invest.

The policies and strategies adopted by firms towards investment and manufacturing significantly affect their ability to adopt technical change for competitive success. Technical change impinges on the decision to invest in new equipment in several ways. Technical change in a firm's products may require different, more advanced or precise means of manufacture to meet different or higher quality specifications of the new products. Developments in product design with more standardisation may enable more efficient means of manufacture with longer production runs. Firms which successfully develop standard product designs may therefore invest in new equipment more appropriate to batch or mass manufacturing techniques. Technical change in manufacturing process through greater automation of production and control may enable important productivity and quality benefits. Firms may invest in such processes to obtain the competitive advantages of cost and reliability.

Often product and process technical change are related. For example, it may not be feasible for firms to attempt to manufacture existing non-standardised products using automated manufacturing equipment. In order to be able to adopt an automated process efficiently, firms may first need to redesign their products to obtain the higher degrees of standardisation necessary for longer production runs.

However, the ability or willingness of firms to invest in new equipment is not only determined by the availability of new technology opportunities. A major determinant of the feasibility of introducing new automation equipment is scale of production. Very small volumes of output may make investment in automated production equipment unfeasible. The constraints, however, cannot be sufficiently encompassed in the concept of scale economy barriers proposed by the industrial organisation theorists.

Firms or plants with large outputs can also be inhibited from new investment if they do not adopt appropriate product design strategies, investment perspectives and adequately trained and acknowledged skills. Conversely firms with small outputs can offset or minimise scale disadvantages by adopting appropriate strategies for products, investment and manpower and so may succeed with new investment where larger rivals fail. The disadvantages of small volume are exacerbated if a firm's product ranges are highly differentiated. Throughput is reduced by lack of standardisation. So the cost effectiveness of investment will be low if too wide a variety of products is manufactured or if excessive custom engineering is permitted. This makes investment in automated equipment even less feasible or likely.

Managements' expectations with respect to the period in which they aim for a return on investment and their attitude to the importance of manufacturing engineering in competition, play a most important role in determining the feasibility of investment in advanced technology manufacturing.

Firms with the necessary levels of output which do recognise the benefits of investment in advanced manufacturing technology and which are willing and able to make the necessary adjustments in their products can obtain major production cost and quality advantages in competition. Major reductions in skilled manpower costs can be realised. Product reliability and quality benefits may also contribute to cost advantages. Continuing improvements in product design and reduction in components through greater standardisation, which frequently accompany the adoption of automated techniques, can further contribute to competitiveness.

Firms differ in their awareness and assessment of the advantages of investment in advanced manufacturing technology. Advanced manufacturing equipment requires a much greater capital outlay and a longer period of time to recoup investment, relative to conventional manufacturing equipment. Firms which adopt a short-term profit horizon for decision-making or which are under pressure from shareholders or banks for a quick return on capital may reject advanced manufacturing equipment as unacceptable and invest instead in conventional machinery. The consequence is to lose long-term cost and reliability competitiveness in the interest of short-run returns.

Status of manufacturing

Firms which give a low priority or status to manufacturing engineering compared to product engineering and marketing may be unable or unwilling to recognise the benefits of efficient, cost competitive manufacturing activities in their firms. They may thus be unprepared to allocate the necessary financial and engineering skill resources to advanced manufacturing processes.

Firms with a strong product engineering or marketing orientation may make large capital outlays for investment in product innovation, with manufacturing investment aimed at serving the requirements of the new products or lowering short-term price rather than developing a more competitive manufacturing operation.

The status of manufacturing engineering is thus a major factor in the awareness of firms of the importance of technical change in manufacturing process for international competitiveness.

Integrated corporate structure: economies of scope

Economies of scope have been largely ignored in the mainstream literature. Contestability theorists have drawn attention recently to its importance but a realistic treatment was constrained by their narrow conceptual formulation. Economies of scope may confer major competitive advantages, particularly in those industries significantly affected by technical change.

Technical change and new commercial developments may create unique opportunities for firms which are a part of integrated industrial groups. This has been demonstrated in several industries which have received significant impact from the diffusion of microelectronic technology. Studies by the author of the television, computer and machine-tool industries found important advantages to firms which were vertically integrated to semiconductor components and/or to manufacturing equipment products.

Firms which are integrated upstream into electronic components or downstream to final products may be able to enjoy cost and delivery advantages from in-house sources of supply. More importantly, such integrated firms may be able to enjoy the benefits of being able to design components specifically suited to the features and performance they want from their products. This can be achieved by parallel or joint design and development efforts.

In-house component manufacture removes the constraint of designing products around the specifications of standard components which are aimed to serve the widest variety of products and are also available to competitors. In the process of designing and developing components and supporting software, firms may also learn to improve and add new features to their products. Integrated firms may also be able to draw upon advanced central R&D support to assist with solving technical problems and to help identify new technical opportunities ahead of non-integrated rivals.

The benefit of integration may not only be technical or procurement related. Horizontal integration with divisions having a strong market presence or experience in related product areas may assist with adaptation of new or changing market requirements. It can assist with cost sharing of marketing efforts through the use of a common marketing and maintenance network.

Rapid transfer of new technology, learning from parallel development and economies of marketing are less likely between independent firms, each seeking its own competitive objectives, than between divisions within a competently and appropriately managed integrated firm. The potential of new technology developments and marketing expertise can only be effectively and swiftly transferred to the other areas if there is close collaboration between the divisions in the firm, however.

Integrated structures in themselves are insufficient to realise the cross-fertilisation benefits of joint component and final development and common marketing strategies. Unless integrated firms adopt the necessary long-term perspectives, and are managed so as to achieve these advantages, they will not be realised.

Manpower policy

Appropriate manpower hiring, training and deployment is an important factor in competitive success and in the successful adoption of technical change. Firms need to be sure that the necessary level of manpower and combination of skills will be available when required. This is particularly important, but even more difficult in periods of dramatic competitive and technical change.

Technical change in an industry may require a significant change in the skill composition of a firm's workforce. With changing technology, new and untried approaches to technical problems and opportunities may be required for which past experience and solutions may be largely irrelevant. A broader, theoretical background enabling more creative approaches and solutions may become more important in the skill composition of successful firms.

Technical change may also require management to reconsider the skills training of professional and senior managerial manpower. Management may need to acquire a thorough understanding of the implications of the new technology for corporate decision-making and planning; it may also need to reconsider the conventional wisdom in the industry concerning the most appropriate perspectives to adopt for competitive strategy. Major changes may be required in the relative influences of the different functions in the firm if the balance in importance between product engineering, marketing and manufacturing engineering is significantly affected by technical change.

Acknowledgements

Thanks are due to the Longman Group for permission to publish this paper which is derived from: Chapter 1, 'Theoretical Perspectives' in *Telecommunications Industry* by E. Sciberras and B. D. Payne, Longman Group UK Ltd, 1986; Chapter 1, 'Introduction to technical change and international competitiveness' in *Machine Tool Industry* by E. Sciberras and B. D. Payne, Longman Group Ltd, 1985.

References

Abernathy, W. J., and Townsend, P. (1975) 'Technology productivity and process change.' *Technological Forecasting and Social Change* 7.

Abernathy, W. J., and Utterback, J.M. (1975) 'A dynamic model of process and product innovation.' *Omega* 3(6): 639-56.

Carter, C. F., and Williams, B. R. (1957) *Industry and Technical Progress*. Oxford: Oxford University Press.

Freeman, C. *et al.* (1965) 'Research and development in electronic capital goods'. *Nat. Inst. Econ. Rev.* (34).

Nelson, R. R., and Winter, S. G. (1982) *An Evolutionary Theory of Economic Change*. Cambridge, Mass: Harvard University Press.

Sciberras, E. (1977) *Multinational Electronic Companies and National Economic Policies*. Connecticut: JAI Press.

(1982) 'Technical innovation and international competitiveness in the television industry'. *Omega* 10(4)

(1983) 'New competition and technical change in the computer industry'. *Technovation* 2(1).

Sciberras, E., Senkar, P., and Swords-Isherwood, N. (1977).'The theory of the firm, technical change, manpower and competitiveness: some theoretical foundations for industry policy studies.' SPRU mimeo (unpublished).

(1987) *Competition, Technical Change and Manpower in Electronic Capital Equipment: A study of the UK Minicomputer Industry*. SPRU Occasional Paper 8, September.

8. Using information systems and technology to gain competitive advantage

Pat Griffiths

Principal Consultant
DCE Information Management Consultancy
Woking

Information systems and technology (IS & T) have always contributed indirectly towards the competitive success of organisations. In the early 'data processing' years, up to about 1970, their role was in reducing cost and improving the efficiency of operational and administrative processes through previously specified transactions processing, monitoring and reporting systems. Since then, IS & T have been increasingly used to improve business effectiveness. This has been achieved both by integrating operational systems horizontally across organisations and by improving the effectiveness of managers through improved management information. These management information systems (MIS) are less likely to be specified in detail than their predecessors. They deliver improved effectiveness by enabling access to appropriate information, and the capability for analysis and manipulation, thus enhancing a manager's ability to plan, control, budget and forecast.

We live in an increasingly competitive age, and since the beginning of the 1980s, a new and different era of computing has emerged, which treats information as a competitive weapon, and focuses on exploiting IS & T for competitive advantage. The aim of the new era is to improve the competitive performance of an organisation in a direct manner, and usually in doing so, the business changes significantly. There may be a change in its intrinsic character; or the scope of the business may be extended; or IS & T may provide powerful leverage to alter the balance between the organisation and its pressure groups (competitors, suppliers and customers). The competitive information systems (CIS) which characterise this era have not replaced DP and MIS systems, but supplement them, and in many cases derive from them.

This new and sometimes dramatic role for IS & T is only achieved when the IS & T strategy is firmly linked to and aligned with the organisation's business strategies. In addition, the business must acknowledge and welcome this new central role, and the technical people must step back from the technology in order to understand and move towards the real needs of the business.

In considering the use of IS & T for competitive advantage, this paper addresses the following interlinking topics:

1. The CIS era and its characteristics.
2. Planning for competitive advantage and determining priorities.
3. Making the most of existing systems.
4. Gaining and maintaining a competitive edge.

The CIS era and its characteristics

The maturity and experience of IS departments determines to a large extent the role played by IS & T. In addition, the evolution of IS & T into the CIS era has been influenced by a number of other factors such as:

1. Growing competition.
2. Other external pressures - economic, legal, political.
3. Enormous advances in computing and communications technology.
4. Rapidly reducing price-performance ratio.

One serious barrier to effective application of IS & T in a business is the lack of understanding between business people and IS & T professionals. The former need to acquire a greater awareness of the role of IS & T in supporting and enhancing business objectives. They also need to be involved in IS & T decision-making processes. On the other hand IS & T professionals need a sound business knowledge so that they can understand the implications of information and its technologies on the business.

I cannot, in this short chapter, trace the evolution from IS & T as an overhead expense to information as a key resource, and IS & T fulfilling a more vital, central role in business. Instead I want to concentrate on the characteristics of competitive information systems (CIS) and how they differ from traditional systems.

Whilst CIS are designed to have a direct impact on the business, they are not necessarily complex, and it is quite likely that they may be built on to existing systems. They are especially dependent on communications and on linking into external organisations such as suppliers and customers, or third party value-adding carriers. Whereas data processing can be characterised as automation of business processes and MIS as providing management support and control, systems for competitive advantage essentially deliver value to the business.

There are a number of characteristics of CIS that have been observed from a survey of some 150 cases. They are described by Ward (1988).

CIS	**Traditional IS&T approaches**
1. External focus-on customers, suppliers, competition and other outside bodies.	Focus on internal processes.
2. Adding value - differentiation through better products or services.	Cost reduction.
3. Sharing the benefits - within the organisation and with customers or suppliers; even with competitors through appropriate strategic alliances.	Localised benefits.
4. Understanding customers needs and delivering value and solutions to problems.	Solving internal problems.
5. Business-driven innovation without emphasis on the latest technology.	Technology-led development.
6. Incremental development-stepped approach, often by 'trial and error', or prototyping.	Total system defined and developed.
7. Exploiting the information to develop the business - for example, by market segmentation.	No exploitation beyond initial system.

Planning for competitive advantage

The achievement of competitive advantage through IS & T is dependent on:

1. Establishing an appropriate environment.
2. Identifying high impact opportunities through planning.
3. Implementing the resultant justified projects, which may be systems, architecture, organisation, technology.

In an enterprise where IS & T are recognised as important factors in competitive strategy, then the environment will provide:

1. A clear corporate strategy, and business unit strategies onto which IS & T strategies can be built.
2. The recognition of information itself as a key resource, commitment from top management for its utilisation as such, and direction of IS & T at board level.
3. A business climate that is conducive to fostering innovation, and in which appropriate IS & T opportunities can be identified and exploited.
4. An organisational structure and culture which is flexible enough to accommodate the changes that may result from implementing new business practices or services based on IS & T, or new IS & T policies and plans directed towards closer linkage between business and IS & T.
5. People in both the business and IS & T areas who understand one another and are in sympathy with one another's needs, objectives and responsibilities.

Strategic planning for effective exploitation of IS & T is a complex process. Here, I am describing only one part of the process - the analysis of the business strategy, formulation of objectives and identification of opportunities for adding value. This part of the process takes a top-down, business-led approach, which focuses primarily on obtaining a detailed understanding of the business strategy and objectives, and thus on identifying high-level information needs derived from these.

Another top-down view is obtained through high-level analysis of real and ideal functions and information areas of the business. From this a conceptual business model can be created, which is the framework on which information architectures, functional architectures and information systems can be built.

A third top-down approach which is more relevant in identifying competitive opportunities and is more creative relies on identifying functions where competitive advantage may accrue. Very often these are at critical interfaces, and most often, at the boundaries between the business and its external contacts.

It can only be effectively used in a climate where innovation in all its forms is encouraged, and good ideas can be nurtured and quickly brought to fruition. Good IS & T ideas are more likely to arise and be taken up in an environment where there is already a sound foundation of co-operation between users, IS & T people and top managements and where IS & T are already treated as central to the organisation. Certain techniques are helpful here to indentify, analyse and prioritise such opportunities.

1. *Value chain analysis* The concept of the value chain is described by Porter in his book *Competitive Advantage* (1985). He suggests that the technique can be used to analyse a firm's position in the external

value chain which comprises the supplier, the company, the distribution channel and the customer, and in its own internal value chain. The internal value chain comprises primary activities, such as obtaining raw materials, processing and disposing of products, sales and marketing, and service. It also includes secondary activities like procurement, technology development (R & D), human resource management, and the provision and maintenance of the firms infrastructure. In the competitive edge context, value chain analysis is used to identify the activities, which become critically important in a competitive strategy and which are dependent on the firms basic business strategy. The potential for improving their contribution in a competitive sense, through improving the information content of the product or service or the information links or flows, can then be assessed.

2. *Customer resource life-cycle (CRLC)* Another vehicle for analysing business functions relating to customer interfaces is the CRLC, which was first documented by Ives and Learmouth (1984). This decomposes the life-cycle associated with the interface activities between supplier and customer into four primary activities and thirteen detailed activities. In a similar way to using the value chain, CRLC can be used to pinpoint critical stages in the life-cycle where potential for competitive advantage can be built - for example, in improving the supplier's capacity to help potential customers decide on them as supplier; to differentiate themselves through superior service, or (as in many examples) through introducing sophisticated on-line ordering facilities. Further details about CRLC and the value chain are given in a paper by Rumble (1987), in which several examples are cited to illustrate competitive systems that could have been exposed through these analyses.
3. *Other techniques in top-down planning* The identification of critical success factors is another well tried technique, introduced by Rockart (1979). It is a widely used and effective technique since, by definition, it focuses on factors which are vital for successfully meeting objectives, or for ensuring optimal effect from business functions.

Making the most of current support

In most large organisations there has been a massive investment in traditional systems. Competitive-advantage systems may be totally independent, but they are more likely to have some dependence on existing systems. It is therefore necessary to evaluate the coverage of business functions by existing systems and their contribution to business objectives. It is also helpful to assess if they provide a valuable basis on which to build CIS. This evaluation could usefully be started in an effectiveness review of the IS & T function, conducted by IS & T people who may be seeking to upgrade the role of their function in the organisation. Its objective may be to obtain management understanding of the role of IS & T, and commitment to strengthening it.

There are several models which may be useful in this process of evaluating value and coverage. They include:

1. McFarlan's 'application portfolio analysis' (McFarlan 1984) which categorises an organisation's IS & T application portfolio into a two-by-two matrix. One axis represents the strategic impact of existing systems, the other the strategic impact of the development and future portfolio.
2. Sullivan's 'environmental analysis' (Sullivan 1985) which determines the degree of infusion of technology into the key operational and strategic functions of the business, and the degree of diffusion of technology (in the form of micros, minis and departmental computing) throughout the organisation.

Ward has paid considerable attention to extending the use of models in this area. He has extended the use of the two-by-two matrix into a comprehensive method for classification of IS & T applications and as a basis for strategic management of the applications portfolio (Ward 1987).

Gaining an advantage through IS & T

Having looked very briefly at the characteristics of CIS, and the environment and procedures for locating innovative opportunities, I would now like to examine some examples of gaining an advantage through IS & T. Competitive strategy and its relationship with IS & T has been written about and researched widely. Much of the work in this field stems from Porter's work (1980, 1985). There is little doubt that IS & T have already had a very far reaching effect on business and competitive activity, and that this influence will continue to grow.

Porter and Miller (1985) propose that the influence of IS & T has been so far reaching as to alter fundamentally the rules of competition in three particular ways:

1. The industry structure is changing.
2. New industries are being created.
3. IS & T are being used as a direct lever to create competitive advantage.

Changing the industry structure

Changes to the structure of industries as a result of the application of IS & T have become evident in a number of industries, and these have had a significant effect on the prevailing rules of competition. Amongst those most profoundly affected are financial services, the travel and holiday industries, and suppliers of information. In these cases, the information content of the products or services themselves are high, and the linkages between buyer and supplier are heavily dependent on communicating information.

Financial services have undergone profound changes. The barriers that separate the different players in this sector - the banks, building societies, insurance companies, stockbrokers and so on, have been severely eroded. In part this has happened as a result of deregulation, but also through increased competition and the encroachment of technology. In addition, new players from outside the traditional financial scene are now active in several fields. For example, some retail stores now offer a range of financial services to their customers. Remote banking is one example of a change in the structure of banking. It has not had a deeply felt influence as yet, although the number of companies offering such facilities is growing. In the UK the Nottingham Building Society was the pioneer, with its Homelink service, which began operating in 1983. It was a brave innovation, but sadly not a conspicuous commercial success. This was basically due to three factors. First, it was pioneering something brand new. Second, the market-place was not very receptive, and third, the scope was severely limited to PRESTEL users. Since then, the Bank of Scotland and TSB have started offering remote banking facilities. Some thirty or more French banks offer a similar service. In the USA, the massive Chase Manhattan Bank has begun a remote banking service. At about the same time that it opened, a survey of the banking field in the USA was conducted. It concluded that 15 per cent of the depositors base was vulnerable to being replaced by home banking and warned decision makers to ignore that at their peril.

Creating new business

The second way in which IS & T are seen to have impacted the rules of competition is where new businesses are springing up in many areas. These are seen as a direct result of opportunities offered by IS & T. They often emerge as new ventures within existing organisations. Various electronic mail services have been set up as additional businesses within large organisations, with close links between the various businesses involved. For example, Telecom Gold from British Telecom. Other new businesses have been set up as a result of the dramatic increase in the demand for information. Companies such as Reuters or Dunn and Bradstreet have responded by setting up on-line information services. Others provide services to specialised markets and rely on collecting information from widespread sources, manipulating it and re-presenting it to the market. Citicorp's Global Financial Reports is an example of this type of service.

Another example of the way in which businesses have stemmed from within existing organisations is where excess internal capacity has provided opportunities. Sears, the giant US company used its expertise in processing credit card accounts and spare capacity within its huge IT resource to provide similar services for other organisations. Eastman Kodak offers long-distance voice and data transmission service on its network, where it has excess capacity.

IS & T as a lever

The third way in which the rules of competition are affected is where IS & T are being applied directly to achieving competitive advantage. This is where IS & T are used as weapons to combat competitive forces, or to act directly in support of the business strategy. This may mean either locking in customers or building barriers to keep out competition. It may also mean minimising operational costs or enhancing differentiation, depending on the business strategy being followed.

There are numerous examples of the use of IS & T as a lever including the following:

Thomson Holidays Their TOPS systems is a videotex-based booking system for use by travel agents. The system is simple to use - viewing, selecting and booking holidays swiftly and efficiently. It has helped to extend Thomson's lead as the UK's biggest packaged holiday supplier. Its competitors have been forced to follow the TOPS sign-on protocols and screen handling routines which have therefore become a de facto industry standard.

Rolls Royce The aero-engine manufacturer, Rolls Royce, has introduced a very sophisticated computer-aided manufacturing (CAM) system. Its aim was to cut production time from twenty-six weeks to six weeks, while at the same time slashing work-in-progress costs by two-thirds.

The VBA, Aalsmeer The Verenigde Bloemenveilingen is a flower auction co-operative based in Aalsmeer, just outside the Schiphol airport in Amsterdam. It is presented as an example of the successful use of both IS and IT as separate components in achieving a World Number One status for a rather unlikely organisation, namely a growers' co-operative, operating in a rather unlikely sector for IT exploitation, in a small country. And yet the VBA runs Europe's largest commercial building, 75 acres in extent and still expanding. It auctions off over 10 million flowers and 1 million potted plants each morning and has an annual turnover of more than 3 billion flowers valued at $500 million. It dominates the Dutch flower export trade, which in total supplies over 60 per cent of the world's exported flowers, to New York and Tokyo amongst other places. The advantage is gained by lowering costs in critical parts of the value chain, enhancing differentiation through the supply of sales statistics and pricing trend reports to growers, and thus attracting greater market share and improved prices.

BMW BMW has introduced a car-ordering and assembly-line control system, which enables customised cars to be built on the same assembly line without disruption of normal production. In contrast to, say, General Motors, which still manufactures mostly for stock and tries to anticipate customers likely preferences for colour schemes and optional extras, BMW manufactures overwhelmingly to individual orders. Apart from being more responsive to customer's wishes, it enables BMW to be more flexible and cuts down on finished car inventory costs both at the factory and at dealers.

Merrill Lynch The firm's cash management system swept clients' overnight surplus funds into the money market, to earn interest, and attracted $8 billion extra investment in a short time. They now have $85 billion under this programme, 70 per cent of the market.

McKesson Corporation McKesson Corporation's experience as a drug wholesaler illustrates the tendency for customers, in this case retail pharmacists, to consolidate their orders with a favoured distributor who put an ordering and distribution channel into place on retail premises. McKesson was subsequently able to sell its usage analysis data to both pharmacists and drug manufacturers, improve its central inventory management and process claims for payment on medical insurance companies, becoming the third-largest insurance claims broker in the USA.

Chance or planning

Whilst the amount of evidence citing examples of competitive advantage is substantial, it is not obvious how the companies identified the opportunities, or how they planned to exploit them as part of an overall IS & T strategy. With the benefit of hindsight, and the documented research findings of several eminent academics and practitioners, it is tempting to assume that most of the examples of successful exploitation were carefully planned. In reality, it is very unlikely that this was so.

Sustaining the advantage

However the advantage has been gained, it is equally important to ensure that it can be sustained and consolidated. It would be very short-sighted and unwise to rush into the introduction of a system that can be easily copied. On the other hand, the effort entailed in introducing a system may have been very considerable, and so it is essential that it presents a formidable obstacle to potential competitors. In the first place, it may take a significant time to put into place the infrastructure that supports the upfront competitive system. Furthermore, if it is a system that has caught the competition unawares, then there is likely to be a gap before they come up with something that will overtake the front runner.

What is of paramount importance is that the total system must maximise the opportunity. Whilst it might have been innovative to put terminals into customers' premises to enable them to order directly, it would have been very easy to copy that use of technology. The essence of a successful competitive system is one which alters the balance of the competitive forces. For example, terminals offered to customers, together with systems that give a substantial advantage to those customers (e.g. financial administrator system to agents) are much more likely to lock in the customer than just the technology on its own. From the customer's point of view it should be advantageous to stay loyal, or be expensive and inconvenient to change.

Another step in maximising the advantage is taken if the information in the system itself can be used to improve marketing, and provide better information into the value chain, thus improving customer service. The 'frequent flyer' and other special programmes initiated by United Airlines are examples of using the information to increase the competitive edge. Another is provided by Sears, who use their massive volume of information on a large proportion of the population in the USA, for selective marketing. Further means of extending the advantage can be found when the system facilities can be reused. Sears, again, sell excess credit card-processing facilities.

The cost and risk of leaving the company vulnerable to leapfrogging is illustrated by the experience of Carrier and Trane. They both operate in the air conditioner original equipment supply market-place. The case centered on their offers to assist architects design and specify equipment. Carrier offered a postal-based design system. Trane came back with an improved system, and took over the lead in the race. Carrier then had to invest heavily in on-line systems to regain the leading position. In this case not only did they have to find a further innovative approach but were forced to invest substantially to make up their lost position.

Summary

A few examples have been given to illustrate CIS. Some have come about through chance and others through meticulous planning and forceful exploitation. No matter how they arise, it is important to have the right environment and culture in place - and then to set about maximising the chances of finding and exploiting ideas through careful planning and implementing appropriate infrastructure or priority systems. Having found the potential opportunities, the advantages must be protected and exploited to the full by applying not only systems and technology but also by extracting maximum benefit from the information entering the system.

References

Griffiths, P. M. (1987) *Information Management in Competitive Success: State of the Art Report*. Oxford: Pergamon Infotech.

Ives, B., and Learmouth, G. P. (1984) 'The information system as a competitive weapon.' *Communications of the ACM,* December.

McFarlan, F. W. (1984) 'Information technology changes the way you compete.' *Harvard Business Review,* May-June: 93-103.

Porter, M. E. (1980) *Competitive Strategy:- Techniques for Analysing Industries and Competitors*. New York: Free Press.

(1985) *Competitive Advantage: Creating and Sustaining Superior Performance* . New York: Free Press.

Porter, M. E., and Miller, V. E. (1985) 'How information gives you competitive advantage'. *Harvard Business Review,* July-August.

Rockart, J. F. (1979) Chief executives define their own data needs.' *Harvard Business Review,* March-April: 81-93.

Rumble, D. (1987) 'Using communications for competitive advantage' in P.M. Griffiths, (ed.) *Information Management in Competitive Success : State of the Art Report*. Oxford: Pergamon Infotech.

Sullivan, C. H. (1985) 'Systems planning in the information age.' *Sloan Management Review,* Winter: 3-12.

Ward, J. F. (1987) *Information Systems and Technology Application Portfolio Management : An Assessment of Matrix Board Analyses*. Cranfield School of Management.

(1988) *Defining Information Systems Strategies (DISS): Teaching Notes*. Cranfield School of Management.

9. The IT people: their qualifications, skill acquirement, and management

Finn Borum

Institute of Organisation and Industrial Sociology
Copenhagen School of Economics
and Social Sciences
Denmark

In relation to the production of software and services for information technology (IT), the human resources, their development and organisation are key issues. This chapter addresses these important questions. It is based upon preliminary findings from the CHIPS project, in which an analysis of the evaluation of actors and organisations within the Danish IT field is being undertaken. The data are restricted to Denmark. A study of the professionals and qualifications of the IT field within the EEC currently being launched, will provide comparative data from several countries. The ICON (International Computer Occupations Network) projects initiated by Andrew Friedman have already led to the generation of cross-national comparisons of computer departments. These include information on several of the dimensions dealt with in this paper.

To facilitate interpretation of the findings, a few important aspects of the Danish context must be mentioned. First, Denmark has a small, open economy where the international influence within IT has been and still is strong. Multinationals (of which IBM is by far the most important) account for the largest share of the IT market, and the Danish IT industry is of modest size within hardware, but important as to software and services. Second, in general Danish enterprises are predominantly small and medium sized, but this applies to a lesser degree in IT, as there has been a tendency towards concentration on the supplier side, and for the user to be above average size. Third, the total size of the Danish labour force (defined as the population in the age group of 16 - 66 years) is 3.5 million. Of these only around 20,000 are IT people as defined here. Fourth, there is a heavy concentration of IT people in the Copenhagen area, where 61 per cent are located. This has to be contrasted with the geographical location of the total labour force, of whom only 23 per cent are located in the Copenhagen area.

Furthermore, mobility of IT people between the western (Jutland) and eastern (Copenhagen area) regions seems to be very modest.

The IT people and their historical development

A comparison of the surveys (Table 9.1) carried out by Denmark's Statistical Bureau (DS) gives a picture of the private sector. It

Table 9.1 The development of the IT population 1970-86: private sector

	1970 Total	1973 Total	1975 Total	1981 Total	1986 Total
Edp manager[a]	236	228	276	307	568
Systems manager	137	136	129	158	237
Programming managers	113	70	62	92	117
Systems consultant	*	*	*	463	1,916
Systems planner	702	593	676	1,204	1,511
Systems programmers[b]	*	324	441	506	1,001
Analyst/programmer	*	*	*	12	1,284
Programmer	1,190	1,211	1,375	1,466	2,261
Analysis and programming	2,378	2,562	2,959	4,208	8,895
Operations manager	154	161	155	79	215
Operations planner	124	217	300	392	651
Operator[c]	1,032	1,135	1,260	1,162	2,114
Data entry supervision	187	159	164	142	116
Data entry operator	2,283	1,948	2,087	1,122	875
Other	567	621	837	-	-
Operations	4,347	4,421	4,803	2,897	3,971
Total	6,725	6,803	7,762	7,105	12,866

* job category not listed in the statistics at that time.

(a) Edp managers are very often responsible for both analysis and programming and operations.

(b) In some locations they are placed among operations staff.

(c) This category includes the following job titles that have appeared in the statistics as indicated.

	1970	1973	1975	1981	1986
Operator	x				
Machine operator		x	x	x	x
Shift supervisor		x	x		
Console operator				x	x
Operators assistant					x

should be noted that the private sector includes from 1981 the two large service bureaux Datacentralen and Kommunedata serving the public sector, and thus defined accounts for about 90 per cent of the total number of IT people.

From this it appears that the IT population has almost doubled in size between 1970 and 1986. This growth, however, covers two opposite developments. Thus the IT people occupied with 'analysis and programming' has almost quadrupled, while the category of 'operations' has been reduced by 10 per cent over the period - after a slight increase during the first five years.

Of those working in analysis and programming, three new job titles have appeared since 1970. The first one to appear in 1973 - systems programmers - indicates a technical specialization of a segment of the programmers in operative systems, data bases, communication networks and so on. It is within this technical core group that we still find programming of special parts of the system in low-level languages, whereas programmers today utilise problem-oriented languages.

The second is system consultants (1981). This may have two explanations, the first of which relates to the need to create a possibility to promote systems analysts, and to circumvent obstacles to salary increases by the creation of a new job title. Another explanation may be a differentiation of systems analysis into more consultancy/sales-oriented functions, and into genuine programming (specification) functions. Data from previous studies (Borum and Enderud 1981) point to the latter explanation, whereas data from the CHIPS project brings both explanations into the picture.

Third, the new mixed category of analyst/programmers (listed for the first time in 1982) reflects a trend to depart from the classical division of labour between systems planning (analysis) and programming (Borum 1987c). This development is supported both by the more powerful programming tools available today, and the mixed experiences with the more classical Taylorist-inspired work organisation.

Table 9.2 takes a closer look at differences in the growth rate of different main categories within the analysis and programming category. It appears that the managerial group has been increasing below the average growth rate. This may partially be caused by the general trend within the IT field to rely more upon project organisation and ad hoc leadership than upon classical hierarchical forms of organisation (Friedman and Cornford 1987; Borum and Enderud 1981). Another complementary as well as competing explanation might be that the category of systems consultants and systems analyst conceals an intermediary managerial layer:

Table 9.2 Comparative growth of IT occupations

Index: 1970=100

Manager:	Edp manager Systems manager Programming manager	100	190
Systems consultant, systems planner		100	488
Systems programmer		100	274
Analysis and programming		100	374
Operations manager		100	140
Operations planner		100	525
Operators		100	205
Data-entry supervisor		100	62
Data-entry operator		100	38
Operations		100	91
Total		100	191

that of senior people with managerial positions and permanent project management responsibilities.

Systems consultants/planners is the group that shows the most important growth rate, whereas programmers and systems programmers come out below average - which indicates that the expected automation of programming is becoming effective. However, this picture is weakened and changed to average growth, if we add the mixed group of analyst/programmers to the programmers and systems programmers.

Turning to operations, two new groups have appeared during the period examined: console operators and operators assistants, that, however, in Table 9.1 have been truncated in the operator category. Two groups have disappeared: the shift supervisors (included in operators in the table) and 'other' personnel. The shift supervisors can be regarded as replaced by operations planners and console operators, while the group 'other' presumably has been eliminated, as we take this category to cover data preparators and technicians. The reduction by 9 per cent of operations staff generally reflects the automation effect and the integration of certain functions in user jobs. The group 'other' has been eliminated from the installations, and the data entry personnel have been reduced to almost a third of the initial population size. The group 'operators' has been increased by a factor of two, which, if compared with the number of installations and the amount of data processed certainly would turn out to be a modest increase. The strongest growth rate belongs to the operation planners (more than a factor of five), which throws the factor two growth of the operators in relief.

The division of labour

Data from the CHIPS project indicate that the classical division of labour between systems analysts and programmers has been eroding away. Specialists that are labelled 'programmer' in many cases actually turn out to be doing both programming and systems analysis. The first observations of this phenomenon were made in small to medium-sized dp-departments and software houses, where our initial reaction was to explain it as a consequence of this division of labour being too inflexible for that size of organisation.

However, later on the same observations were made in large installations as well as in the case of a very large service supplier Datacentralen, which furnishes the Danish public sector with data-processing and software. This does not mean that the division of labour is not more elaborate in large than small organisations. In fact, in the just-mentioned large organisation, all the job categories depicted in Figure 9.1 from Ehn and Sandberg (1979) can be found.

Figure 9.1 The deskilling of DP workers (*source*: Ehn and Sandberg 1979)

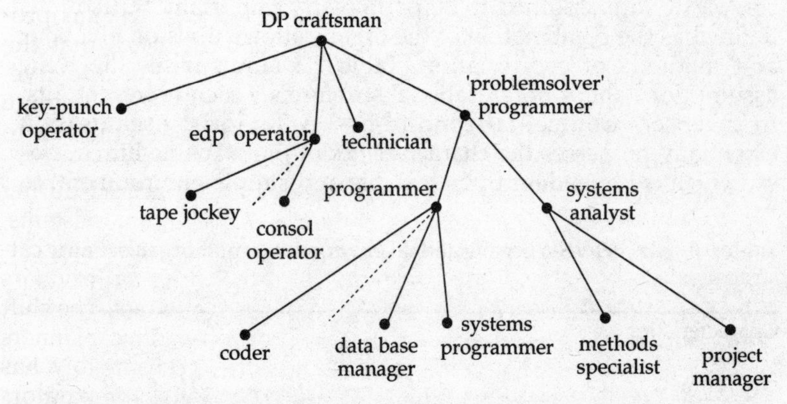

But our findings contradict the deskilling hypothesis put forward by several authors in the 1970s (Greenbaum 1976; Ehn and Sandberg 1979; Borum 1977), who assumed that the specialists employed within the planning functions related to IT, would also in due time be the victims of a vertical and horizontal specialisation. Job enlargement and flexible partition of tasks, and not deskilling, is the impression of the development of the Danish IT specialists.

The organisational structures

A dominant trend within the organisational structures of the IT field is the utilisation of project organisation or customer-based departments as the standard organisational response to the task environment. These project groups comprise a mixture of programmers and programmers/planners, and the distinction between the two groups is mainly that of seniority or formal qualifications: many of the specialists start as programmers, and then in a couple of years they develop into mixed programming/planning functions.

This clear deviation from more Taylorist organisation/principles may be understood by means of contingency theory, which stipulates that, in order to be effective, organisational structures must 'fit' important contingency factors of which two are environment and technology.

Organisational structures as a response to the environment

Accordingly to Mintzberg (1979) one of the important factors upon which the organisational structure is contingent is the environment, where the two environmental dimensions of stability and complexity are assumed to be particularly important. Structure is defined as the combination of the organisation's division of labour and methods of coordination. Table 9.3 summarises the basic assumptions about organisational structures which represent 'fits' to given environmental conditions. A Taylorist organisation essentially possesses the characteristics of the machine bureaucracy, which is dependent upon a stable and simple environment. In

Table 9.3 'Fits' between organisational environments and organisational structures

Characteristics of environment	Stable	Dynamic
Complex	Professional bureaucracy (standarisation- of skills)	Adhocracy (mutual adjustment)
Simple	Machine bureaucracy (standardisation of work processes)	Simple Structure (direct supervision)

other words, the machine bureaucracy is geared towards mass production and not the present production mode within the IT field.

What might explain the erroneous 'deskilling forecasts' perceptions earlier cited is the fact that they were made around the end of the 'main-frame-era', just before the minis had acquired importance. Thus the forecasts projected the features of existing large installations, at that time operating in stable environments, into future tendencies. Technological development in the shape of minis and later on PCs, and the post-industrial societal development, however, lead to quite changed environmental conditions: dynamism and complexity. In order to cope with this, resort has to be taken to either complex actors (the professional bureaucracy) or complex strucutres (the adhocracy) or a combination thereof.

Information technology as a contingency factor

The above line of reasoning leaves us with a need to understand information technology itself as a contingency factor. How does it shape the work situation of IT-specialists, and what pressures does it exert towards certain modes of division of work and co-ordination? To answer these questions, Woodward's (1965) distinction between unit, mass and process production is useful.

Woodward found that unit production - which comprises production according to customers' order, prototypes, and small batches - essentially represented a craft culture built around skilled workers working in small groups in close contact with their supervisor. In short, the structures found were organic. In contrast to this, mass production which produced large batches were machine-bureaucracies, characterised by a high degree of formalisation and the employment of unskilled workers. The picture shifted again significantly when moving to process production, where an organic structure was found, manned by skilled workers maintaining the system, and by specialists overseeing the production. The production process *per se* had been automatised, that is the heavy routine operations removed from the domain of the workers.

If we compare the work of edp specialists with these categories, it is *unit production* which comes closest to the task and structural characteristics of software and service production. Production to customers' order has been the main feature of Danish IT-specialists, both when employed in internal dp departments, in software houses and in service bureaux. No mass production of software has yet developed, and craftsmanship, described as the skills one develops through around two years of practical work as a programmer/analyst, is the core upon which the organisational structure is based.

In larger installations and service bureaux a certain resemblance with process production is found: the surveillance, maintenance and modification of the systems in operation require the employment of skilled programmers/analysts and specialists in the form of systems programmers, LAN (local area network) specialists and so on, who in many cases hold a university-level degree.

To this picture can be added the development of increasingly powerful software (operative systems and fourth-generation tools and languages) and easy test and debugging facilities, which to a certain extent remove the more routine task elements from the programmers/analysts' jobs. The resulting future development will most likely not be one of mass production, but one of skilled workers (programmers/analysts) working within organic-type structures.

The qualifications and skill acquirement

DS' 1970 survey provided information on the IT people's educational background (Table 9.4). Two characteristics of this table are important. The variety of formal qualifications and the low proportion of academics within edp in the early years. The variety may be explained as the consequence of the educational systems' inability to provide obvious candidates for vacant positions within this new occupational field, and the absence of established norms and traditions for recruitment and selection of applicants. The low proportion of academics can be regarded as a consequence of the lower

Table 9.4 Educational background of the IT population 1970 and 1986 (%)

	1970(DS)	1986(estimated)
High school	22	20
Edp assistant	-	20
'Bachelor' in business economics (HA/HD)	3	5
Short business educations (HH/Merkonom)	1	10
Engineers or other technical educations	4	5
University degree or equivalent (inclusive of computer science	0	10
Other	70	30
	100	100

level of academics produced by the educational system then, and the educational institutions' orientation towards more traditional types of jobs. In addition to this, the firms may have been inclined to attach little importance to theoretical competences and thus were not trying very actively to attract academics.

Since 1970 official Danish statistics do not provide information about the qualifications of the IT people. From other CHIPS data (Strandgaard and Antonsen 1988) we know that the qualification level within the edp field has been increasing. This reflects both the general increase in Danish society's qualification level, and the emergence of education courses which specifically aim at the edp field.

The most significant shift is that today Studentereksamen (high school exam) together with edp-assistant education is the most common educational background. The ratio of academics has also been increasing over time. More university candidates, engineers and business economics are entering the field, and the proportion of other educational background has decreased significantly. But still it is the variety of formal qualifications and the open recruitment policies that characterise the field.

Even within the few large organisations that have developed an internal formalised education for planners, programmers and so on, learning-by-doing still appears to be the primary mode through which IT people acquire their skills. Our data indicate that these processes of skill acquirement resemble those of an artisan mode of production. The more experienced IT specialists pass on to the less experienced their knowledge through collaboration around concrete projects. And this apprenticeship system is controlled by the specialists, who form an autonomous body outside the control of management.

1. *Edp-assistant* The edp-assistant course is a basic public education course aimed at programming and functions. If the student's background is a Studentereksamen (high school exam) or the equivalent, exams can be passed after one year, otherwise two years of study is necessary. Some 3,784 students have graduated over the period 1974-85.
2. *Data engineers* The electro-engineer programme at Danmarks Tekniske Hojskole (The Technical University) consists of four lines, one of which exclusively concentrates on data processing. It is primarily aiming at the hardware side. Approximately forty students graduate each year.
3. *Datalog* During the period 1984-7 ninety-three students graduated in computer science from the universities of Copenhagen and Aarhus. The education is primarily software oriented and aimed at

programming, implementation and maintenance of new systems for research and technical administrative purpose as well as evaluation of new edp-equipment.

4. *Exam. scient.* This title covers datalog students who have passed the first part of the study. Although it is not a final examination the students have been given the above title because a great number of them have not been able to complete their study course owing to insufficient capacity in the second stage. During the years 1980-6, 603 students passed the first part of the study. We know that a small number of them by now have also passed the second part and are thus included in the datalog group. However, many of them never complete their studies, as after having passed the first part, they have found positions in edp organisations.

If we assume that all people with these qualifications work within the IT field, only around 25 per cent of IT people possess a formal IT education.

Recruitment and itineraries

Recruitment to IT specialist functions is increasingly based upon the intake of individuals possessing social or communication skills, or skills within the application area or trade. Thus individuals are often recruited from user departments to internal computer departments and supplier organisations often acquire individuals with formal education or practical skills within customer areas.

This flexibility of recruitment patterns has co-existed with the former very strict distinction between IT specialists and users, which is eroding away. Individuals are increasingly moving across this borderline, and in user departments one finds former IT specialists as managers or serving as important intermediaries between the dp departments and the user departments. Or you find users, who in fact spend most, or an important part of their time, carrying out functions that you would label as IT functions.

The itineraries within the Danish IT field further support flexibility as the characteristic of IT specialists occupying positions as programmers and planners. Even if there is a tendency to recruit persons with higher formal qualifications to positions as planners, it is not possible to establish any strong correlation between the individuals' initial qualifications and positions, and their positions and functions after three years within the IT field.

Strandgaard and Antonsen(1988) in their study only identify two trends: that edp assistants most often are recruited to programming and systems analysis functions and tend to remain within these, whereas university graduates mainly are recruited to systems consulting functions and also tend to stay there. A further sign of the flexibility of career patterns is that the former sharp distinction between 'analysis and programming' and 'operations' seems to be weakened. The positions of systems programmers and systems planners in many organisations are also within reach of persons who start as operators.

The management of IT people

Organisational structures as reflections of management ideology

Ideology in this context denotes a set of beliefs, true or false, about what represents important environmental stimuli and what are adequate responses to perceived environmental conditions. Ideology in this sense reduces uncertainty and complexity for management by offering a perceptional filter towards environmental stimuli and behavioural rules-of-thumb concerning what structural solutions to consider.

The environment does not directly determine the organisational structure. Management ideology intervenes in two ways: first in that management reacts to its perceptions of environment not to objective environmental factors; next in that the structural responses chosen to perceived environmental demands represent what management believes to be adequate measures.

That management ideology is important and has been changing over time, is recognised by several authors, including Mintzberg (1979), who labels it fashion and deals with it as the structure of the day; new structural arrangements appear from time to time and become fashionable. Examples of cultural imports from the USA to Denmark after the Second World War are MBO schemes (management by objectives), and more recently project organisation and divisionalisation, all three of which are much favoured within the IT field.

Taylorism is not only a label for structural solutions chosen by management in a specific historical and spatial context, but also for a managerial ideology that leads management to prefer certain structural solutions to other possible ones. There is ample evidence, as revealed by a recent study of Hull Kristensen (1986) that Taylorism and Fordism do not exist as a strong managerial ideology in Denmark any more. The structural solutions chosen within Danish industry today show a great variation and often what Hull Kristensen labels schizophrenic traits. The three new structural arrangements mentioned above may be considered as further evidence of this abandoning of the Taylorist ideology.

That Taylorism infected the IT field in the 1960s and the early 1970s is evidenced by both prescriptions on how to organise your dp department (see as an example Brandon 1963) and the actual solutions chosen by some of the large installations and service bureaux. However, a comparative study by Friedman and Cornford (1987) shows, that not only in Denmark, but also in other countries, it is difficult to interpret recent managerial practice as Taylorism. Instead a managerial strategy of 'responsible autonomy' appears to be the dominating managerial action towards the IT specialists.

Methods of control as a result of power relations

Power relations in and around organisations are an important contingency factor, which contributes to the explanation of success and fiasco of management's control and co-ordination method in relation to IT specialists. These control measures, and their efficiency in the light of the power relations, can be dealt with by utilising Mintzberg's (1979) co-ordination categories of formalisation and supervision, standardisation of skills, and control of economic performance.

Formalisation and supervision Under this heading fall the measures employed during the early phases of the IT field's development. Methods and standards were implemented (Brandon 1963) that both aimed at making the specialists' production process more transparent and their products more standardised. By imposing standardisation and supervision of the specialists' practice, at least two objectives were pursued. One was to reduce costs, another to reduce the dependency on the individual specialist. By making their working methods conform to certain norms, and their products to certain standards, the expropriation of craft knowledge and the replacement of the individual specialist were obtained.

These measures, that possess quite distinct Taylorist traits, can be regarded as management's immediate efforts to gain control of the new group of specialists via intraorganisational mechanisms. To have a certain amount of control became important as the scope of the information systems grew. Data processing costs represented an important budget item and important segments of the firm's core operating procedures were incorporated in the dp systems. The division of work between programmers and analysts also falls within this repertoire of control measures.

However, these efforts, which essentially deskill the IT specialists, were resisted by the specialists in several ways. One was to leave the organisation if control measures that implied a formalisation beyond the specialists' threshold of tolerance were imposed. In a tight labour market - and that has characterised the Danish IT field until today - this exit-option has been extensively utilised, as can be read from actual labour turnover and the specialists' loyalty towards their craft.

The second type of resistance was to bypass the rules and regulations imposed. This is a common story from the installations with well-developed methods and standards: that they do exist, but are only utilised to a limited extent. This discrepancy between management prescriptions and specialists' actual practice is also reported by Friedman and Cornford (1987). To enforce the rules and methods is time-consuming, difficult, and in most organisations runs counter to the efforts to terminate projects within a tolerable time and resource schedule.

Third, rule enforcement is complicated by the fact that the dp managers and supervisors in nearly all cases are IT specialists themselves. Thus they know the problems connected with strict rule adherence, and perhaps share the craft values of the specialists whom they are supposed to supervise. This third source of resistance can be labelled the lack of internal cohesion of the management system, which tries to control the specialists.

The fourth source of resistance which appears to be specific to the Danish context is the specialists' utilisation of collective strategies. The large public sector service bureaux and important public sector installations formed the platform for the establishment of an edp specialists' independent union (PROSA), which was later followed by the white-collar union's establishment of a computing section (SAM data). These unions include an important share of the IT specialists employed in public organisations, and PROSA has been influential in some of these as to working conditions, wages and participations. They have initiated some strikes (the last one in 1987).

Formalisation and supervision are thus subject to important limitations, which may explain the emphasis put upon the co-ordination methods mentioned below. However, they have not been completely discarded and are still part of the management's repertoire. Even if they are not very efficient measures, they still may be important from a symbolic perspective. They signal that even though the IT specialists have important zones of liberty, they are still subject to management control, and do not form an autonomous, professional community.

Standardisation of skills The introduction of methods and standards described above was intimately linked to the establishment of internal educational systems by which managment tried to develop skills in accordance with organisation requirements. However, the core of the education process remained in the craft-like on-the-job-training, which was only partially controlled by management, and neither solved the problem of supply of IT specialists nor the creation of a labour force with more generally applicable qualifications.

The Danish educational institutions showed a surprisingly low interest in the establishment of supplier-independent IT-education, and were not pushed by the IT specialists. However, important private users and employer associations which wanted to reduce supplier dependencies and to ease the tight labour market, around 1970 initiated public courses within systems analysis and programming. This led to the establishment of a one-year education course (edp assistant) that today is the most important single input source to the IT labour market and constitutes the normal basis for on-the-job training of programmers. Even though this course has been criticised for being poorly geared to the actual tasks of the specialists in large installations, it has secured an important and increasing input of individuals since the mid-1970s.

As to the contents of the education, management has exerted a considerable influence. This was reflected in the recent revision of the edp-assistant education, in which the unions' representatives were out-voted by management and governmental representatives. In the absence of trends to professionalisation, standardisation of skills via the public educational institutions may be both an accessible and efficient way of assuring a certain control of the IT specialists.

Control of economic performance This method of control implies the measurement of output from the IT specialists in economic terms, a (quasi) market mechanism. It is a crude, but in many contexts efficient control measure, which avoids the problems and costs involved in detailed supervision of production processes or products of the specialists.

In the Danish context, this control method has become very popular in management circles since the mid-1970s, as evidenced by the increasing number of edp departments which are separated into profit centres or independent companies, and which are supposed to compete with other possible suppliers of services, both inside and outside the mother corporation.

This method of control is not necessarily an alternative or a substitute to those previously mentioned, but may go hand in hand with them. In relation to a grouping of specialists, who control a complex technology, but do not constitute a collective, this may be one way of allowing them autonomy, but at the same time securing management profitability.

Concluding comments

The analysis of the Danish IT people has clearly demonstrated that we are dealing with a dynamic and complex cluster of occupations, the dynamics of which are only partly identified.

The formal qualifications of the IT people in Denmark are diverse, and only about a fourth of the specialists possess a formal IT-education. This proportion, however, has been increasing importantly since 1970, in line with the creation of formal education directly oriented towards IT positions. To what extent this trend will continue is uncertain. Interviews with managers on different levels reveal that in most cases formal technical qualifications are neither defined as a scarce resource nor as the primary basis of recruitment. Instead emphasis is put on the recruitment of persons with qualifications within the specific trade or application area, or with qualifications that have created a general analytical capability and a flexible mind.

Apparently, managerial recruitment policies contain two different elements. One is to cope with the dynamics of the IT field by attracting flexible or polyvalent actors. The other is to facilitate the interaction between IT people and the organisation's customers/clients by recruiting persons who from their formal background can more easily communicate.

As to the work culture of IT people, it is characterised by a flexible division of labour, project-oriented organisational structures, skill acquirement through artisan-like processes, a high degree of autonomy, and flexible career patterns. This post-Taylorist practice has been explained as a consequence of adaptation to a complex and dynamic environment and the IT technology, and as a result of shifts in management's belief of what represents effective organisation, and in the power relations in and around IT organisation.

With several forces pushing away from more traditional Taylorist modes of organisation, it is not very likely that this trend will change. This brings into focus more 'soft' managerial co-ordination mechanisms as the possible avenue towards effective IT organisation.

This may explain the great interest in cultural management that has characterised the Danish IT field during recent years. Our case studies from the CHIPS project indicate that even though there is a great awareness of the importance of organisational culture, essential problems related to the co-existence of quite different subcultures within the same organisation still need to be tackled. How to manage the differentiation and integration of such different subcultures as operations, technical development, systems development, sales and consultancy within the same IT organisation seem to be a major challenge.

References

Administrationsdepartementet, (1987) *Statens EDB til Administrative Formal* . Copenhagen: Finansministeriet.

Borum, F. (ed.) (1977) *Edb, arbejdsmiljo og virksomhedsdemokrati.* Copenhagen: Nyt fra Samfundsvidenskaberne.

Borum, F. (1980) 'Systems design and scientific management'. *Acta Sociologica,* 23 (4): 287-96.

(1987a) *Computer Specialist Communities: A Paradigmatic Analysis of the Structuring of the Danish Field.* CHIPS working paper. Copenhagen, School of Economics and Social Science.

(1987b) *Organisational Adaptation and Learning within the Field.* CHIPS working paper. Copenhagen, School of Economics and Social Science.

(1987c) *Beyond Taylorism: The IT-specialists and the Deskilling Hypothesis.* CHIPS working paper. Copenhagen: School of Economics and Social Science.

Borum, F. and Enderud, H. (1981). *Konflikter i organisationer: belyst ved studier af edb-systemarbejde.* Copenhagen, Nyt Nordisk Forlag/Arnold Busck.

Brandon, D. (1963) *Management Standards for Data Processing.* New York: Van Nostrand Reinhold.

Braverman, H. (1974) *Labour and Monopoly Capitalism.* New York: Monthly Review Press.

Child,J.,Loveridge,R.,Harvey,J.,andSpencer,A.(1984) 'Microelectronics and the quality of employment in services' in P. Marstrand (ed.) *New Technology and the Future of Work and Skills.* London: Frances Pinter.

Civilokonomen, Lonstatistik 1984, 1985, 1986, 1987.

Danmarks Statistik (1972) EDB-taelling 1970.

(1974) EDB-taelling 1973.

(1975) EDB-taelling 1975.

(1982:1) Lon- og indkomststatistik.

(1987:1) Lon-og indkomststatistik.

Commission of the European Communities, Directorate General for Employment, Social Affairs and Education. *The Software Industry.* Social Europe, supplement 6/86.

Ehn,P.and Sandberg,A.(1979) *Foretagsstyring och lontagarmakt.* Falkoping: Bogforlaget Prisme.

Friedman, A. (1987) *Strategies for Computer People.* CHIPS working paper. Copenhagen, School of Economics and Social Science.

Friedman, A., and Cornford, D.S. (1987) 'Strategies for meeting users demands: an international perspective.' *International Journal of Information Management,* 7: 3-20.

(1988) *Computer Systems Development: An Historical Analysis.* London: Wiley.

Greenbaum, J. (1976) 'Division of labour in the computer field.' *Monthly Review,* 28(3).

Hingel, J. (1985) *Software and Social Change in Denmark.* Institute of Organisation and Industrial Sociology, Copenhagen, School of Organisation and Social Science. Mimeo.

Hull Kristensen, P. (1986) *Teknologiske projekter og organisatoriske processer*. Roskilde: Forlaget Samfundsokonomi og Planaegning.
March, J. G., and Olsen, J. P. (1976) *Ambiguity and Choice in Organisations*. Oslo: Universitetsforlaget.
Mintzberg, H. (1979) *The Structuring of Organisations*. Englewood Cliffs, NJ: Prentice-Hall.
OECD. Information Computer Communications Policy (1985) *Software: an Emerging Industry*. Paris: OECD.
Politikens, EDB Bog. (1985).
Prosa (1986) *EDB-fagets Fremtid*. Copenhagen: Forlaget Probog.
(1984) Note on the edp manpower.
Sam-Data (1986) Lonstatistik. Copenhagen.
Scott, W. (1981) *Organisations: Rational, Natural, and Open Systems*. Englwood Cliffs, NJ: Prentice Hall.
Strandgaard, J., and Antonsen, H. (1988) *Computer Specialists: A Survey*. CHIPS working paper. Copenhagen, School of Economics and Social Science.
Thompson, J. D. (1967) *Organisations in Action*. New York: McGraw-Hill.
Woodward, J. (1965) *Industrial Organisation: Theory and Practice*. Oxford: Oxford University Press.

10. Introducing new technologies in Canada: some human-resource implications

Keith Newton

Senior Research Director
Economic Council of Canada ,Ottawa

Technological change is widely perceived as the key to productivity and international competitiveness. And in a vast country such as Canada with enormous regional differences in resource endowments and industrial structure, and significant disparities in prosperity, new technologies are seen as a means to diversify economic activity and achieve better regional balance.

But technological advance is, itself, uneven, and has the capacity to create both winners and losers. It is important, therefore, to examine the evidence concerning the impact of new technologies on the labour market, since that is the stage on which, for the majority of income earners, adjustment to change is acted out.

Many Canadians have welcomed the new technologies in the workplace. But others have misgivings about the impact of these innovations on their jobs and their incomes. Do the new technologies create jobs or destroy them? Where will the new jobs be? What skills will be needed? Which occupations are in jeopardy? There is much concern but little agreement. Some analysts maintain that we are confronted by a wave of innovation so rapid in its diffusion and severe in its effects that widespread unemployment and deskilled and dehumanised jobs must inevitably result. More optimistic are those who take comfort in the lessons of history, arguing that even truly revolutionary innovations like steam, electricity and the internal combustion engine did not produce massive, pervasive or enduring unemployment. The optimists maintain that the 'information revolution' is simply the latest in a long series of developments that have helped to increase income and employment.

Others are less certain about the overall net impact of technological change, but assert, pragmatically, that there will inevitably be some adjustment problems for particular industries, regions and occupational groups. The essential point, for them, is that we must anticipate the need for policies and programmes to ease the pain of transition. Thus education, training, mobility and social security measures are among the range of their concerns.

Finally, there are those who stress the need to recognise a 'technological imperative'. We have no choice, in this view, but to adopt and adjust to the new technologies as fast as possible. We cannot stem the tide. If we do not advance technologically, our trading rivals surely will, and we stand to lose in terms of productivity, competitiveness and, ultimately, jobs.

There is some truth in all of those arguments. Jobs are both created and destroyed by innovation, and one can think of many examples of each. More difficult, however, is prediction of the impact of any particular new product or process. Equally complex is assessment of the overall impact on the economy. It is clear, however, that change causes imbalances than can, in turn, impair the performance of the economy. It is therefore clearly essential to examine the labour market impacts of technological change.

Employment and income effects

Consider, first, employment. Fig. 10.1 is based on a 'decomposition' analysis that separates out the sources of employment change in Canada in the intercensal decade 1971-81. Two major sources of employment change are depicted in the figure. First, what is

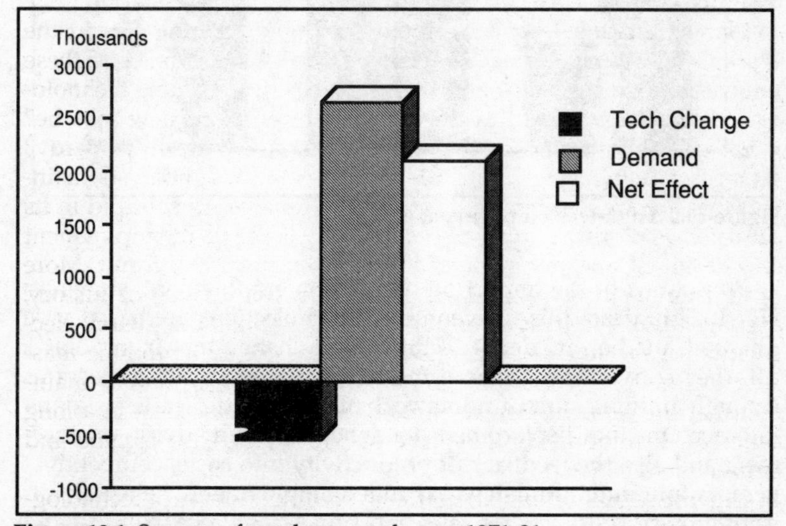

Figure 10.1 Sources of employment change, 1971-81
Thousands of workers

labelled final demand consists of the growth of the overall economy and shifts in the composition of consumption, as tastes change. The second sources, labelled technological change, combines productivity effects and changes in input mix - the production 'recipe' of industry. The results indicate that the technological changes were more than offset by overall expansion of demand in the economy - demand expansion attributable in part to the 'productivity payoff' of technological change. The net effect was job creation of about 2.1 million.

Next, the 'high-tech' sector of Canadian industry (Economic Council of Canada 1987) clearly contributed significantly to this growth (Fig. 10.2). While employment in the overall economy grew at the annual rate of 3.1 per cent per year in 1971-81, the high-tech sector grew at 4.6 per cent. However, the impact of technological change has been uneven in the past, across industries, occupations and regions.

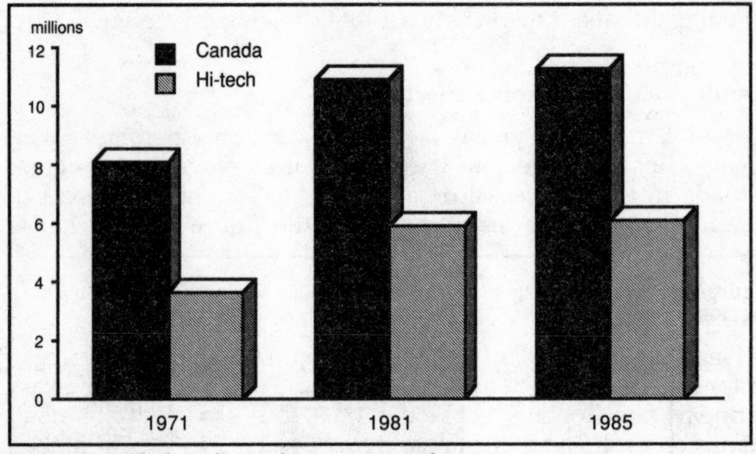

Figure 10.2 High-tech employment growth

Projections of the impact on occupation employment, shown in Fig. 10.3, indicate this unevenness. The projections are based on a unique Canadian model of technological change that incorporates a rather conventional macro model to drive output projections through an input-output framework of the Leontief variety. Taking into account the displacement tendency of productivity enhancement and also the feedback of productivity into costs, competitiveness, output and, ultimately, expanded employment, we see significant growth prospects for sales and professional occupations, and massive job loss for machinery occupations.

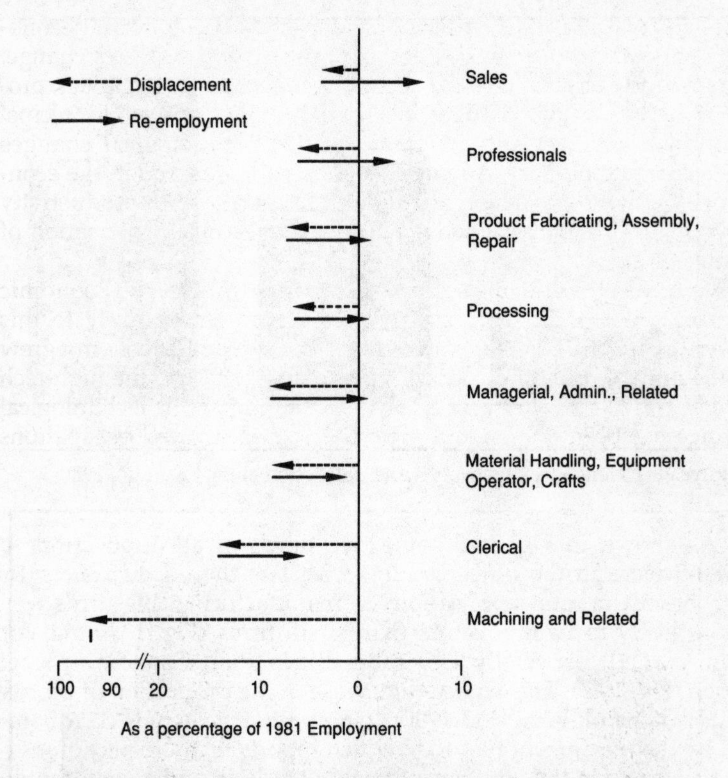

Figure 10.3 Displacement and re-employment in selected occupations, 1981-95

Finally, looking at some results from our survey of 1,000 private sector establishments across Canada, Fig. 10.4 shows that the innovating establishments showed almost the same employment expansion as the non-innovators in the period 1980-5, paid higher wage increases and had much bigger growth in sales.

Innovation in Canada

Much of the information on technological change in Canada is aggregate, indirect or piecemeal. To get a comprehensive snapshot, the Economic Council of Canada conducted a survey of computer-based innovations in 1,000 private sector establishments in the period 1980-5. Applications reported ranged from a single PC for sales analysis to integrated office networks, from automated sewing machines to robot welders, and from statistical process control to CAD-CAM systems.

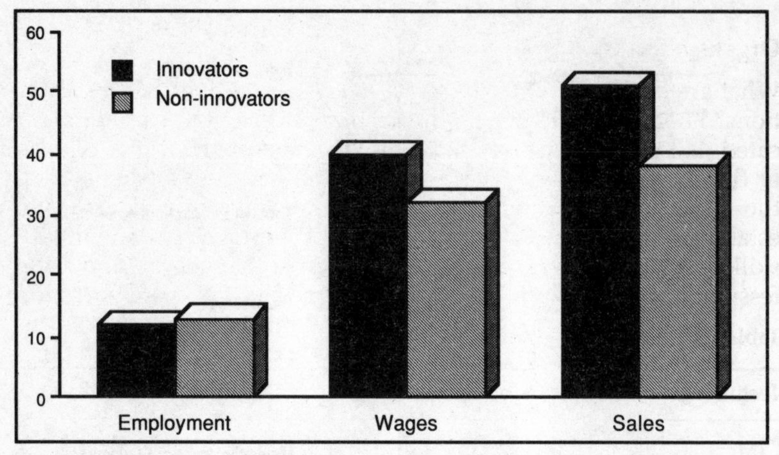

Figure 10.4 Trends in jobs, wages and sales. Percentage change, 1980-5

As shown in Fig. 10.5 some two-thirds of all applications in 1980-5 were in the office setting, with less than a quarter in the higher-cost process applications in manufacturing. Big firms were more likely to be innovators than small firms (Fig. 10.6) and foreign-owned (especially US) more likely than Canadian-owned firms (Fig. 10.7). The expected increase in the proportion of process innovations in the period 1980-5 (shown in Fig. 10.5) is corroborated by the message of Fig. 10.8, which reports firms' expectations of the increases in the numbers of people working with new technologies in the same period.

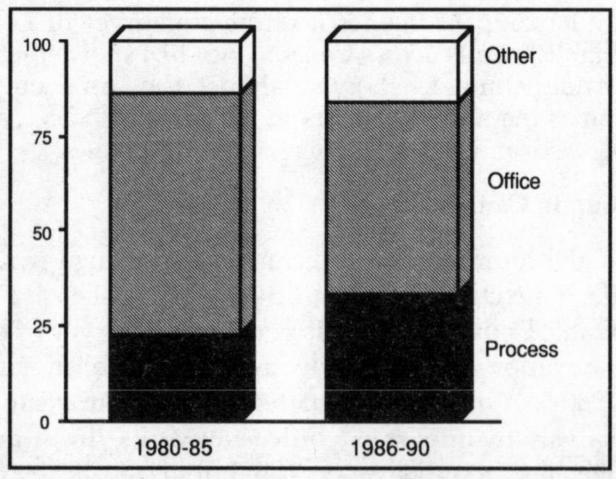

Figure 10.5 The Technologies. Percentage of all innovations reported

Organisation level impacts

What are of the workplace repercussions of technological innovations? First, some 72 per cent of the innovators in our sample indicated that tech change had led to the creation of new types of jobs or the substantial modification of existing ones. A comparison of the occupation structure of innovating versus non-innovating establishments shows a much smaller proportion of manual and skilled blue-collar jobs and larger shares of managerial and professional/technical jobs. Somewhat surprisingly, over a quarter of

Table 10.1 Technology case studies

Technology	Industry	Features
CIM	Aircraft engine mfg	• Socio-technical planning • Semi-autonomous work groups • Pay for knowledge
Robots SPC	Automobile engine mfg	• Training
JIT	Electronic and elec. assembly	• Productivity gain-sharing
CAL A1	Computer services	• High-tech based growth
Office Automation		• Futurist innovations • Relocation • Retraining • Semi-autonomous work groups • Union management committee
Production Automation	Pulp and paper	• Retraining • PlanningVarious
	Various mfg	• Sources of failure
Medical robotics	Rehabilitation research	• Training disabled workers

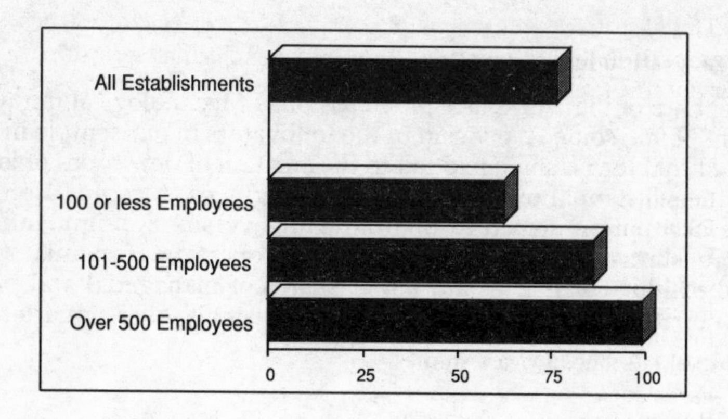

Figure 10.6 The Innovator. Percentage of establisments

the innovators, 28.07 per cent, reported no new skill requirements, but for the remainder, retraining 42.4 per cent, external recruitment 5.17 per cent, or some combination of retraining and external recruitment, 24.57 per cent, were the usual way of meeting new skill needs. As for training, 20.3 per cent of training programmes were of one week or less in duration, 30.4 per cent of two to four weeks, 36.2 per cent of one to six months with 13.1 per cent being of more than six months. That just over half the courses were of less than a month's duration, reflects, perhaps the predominantly office settings of most applications of new technologies. The greater emphasis on process technologies in the future may well mean more sophisticated, lengthier and costlier training programmes.

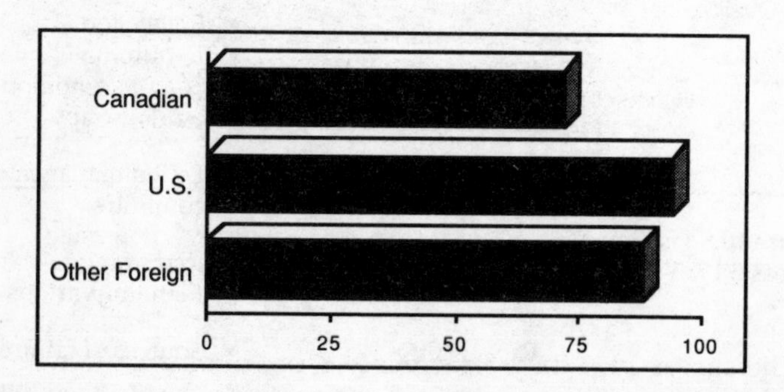

Figure 10.7 The Innovators Percentage of establishments

The vast majority of technological innovators also reported some organisational innovations in the 1980-5 period, and from both the survey results and our case studies we encountered frequent mention of a large variety of 'soft-tech' innovations ranging from quality circles to profit sharing. The names used for these included:

Employee involvement
ESOP: Employee stock ownership plans
Flexitime
Gain-sharing
Industrial democracy
Just-in-time inventory
Organisational effectiveness
Participative decision-making
Pay for knowledge
Quality control circles
Semi-automatic work groups
Quality of working life
Socio-technical systems
Statistical process control
Venture ream

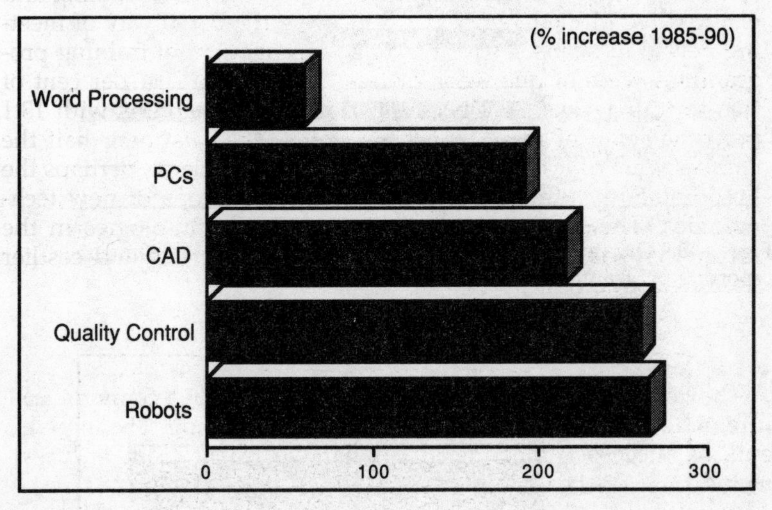

Figure 10.8 Working with selected technologies, 1985-90. Percentage increase, 1985-90

The survey identified three major types of organisational innovation: innovations in remuneration (including profit sharing, gain sharing and pay-for-knowledge); work redesign (including job sharing, job enlargement, autonomous work groups and quality circles) and participative structures such as joint committees (Fig. 10.9). The message of the case studies was convincing on this point: technological change, organisational redesign and innovative human resource policies must go hand in hand. You can't put twenty-first century technology into a nineteenth-century workplace.

The various technologies involved in the case studies, the industries concerned and the particular themes which emerged are shown in Table 10.1

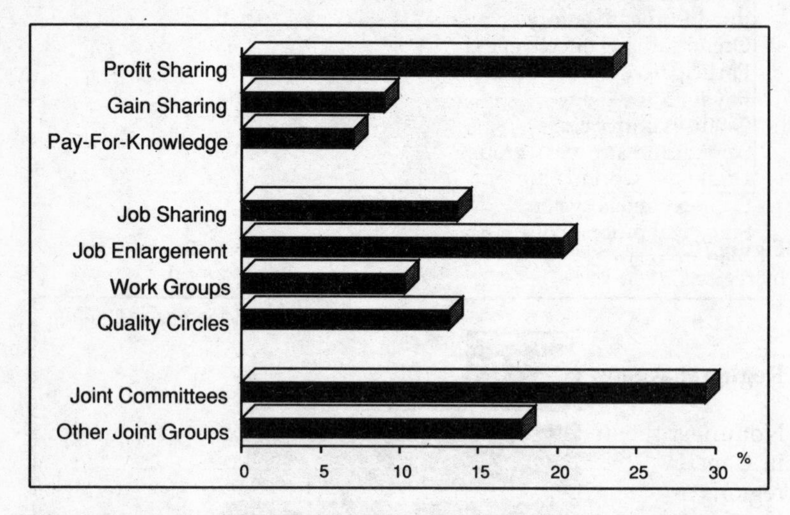

Figure 10.9 Organizational innovations. Percentage of establishments reporting programme

The dominant theme varies from case to case, but a common feature of all the success stories is emphasis on training. The ingredients of success (reflecting also what we learnt from failures) include:

- careful pre-planning of the social and technical aspects;
- active involvement of everyone affected by the change - the stakeholders;
- development of collaborative organisational and work designs;
- strong commitment to the existing workforce;
- the provision of the necessary training in advance of the implementation of change;
- management training.

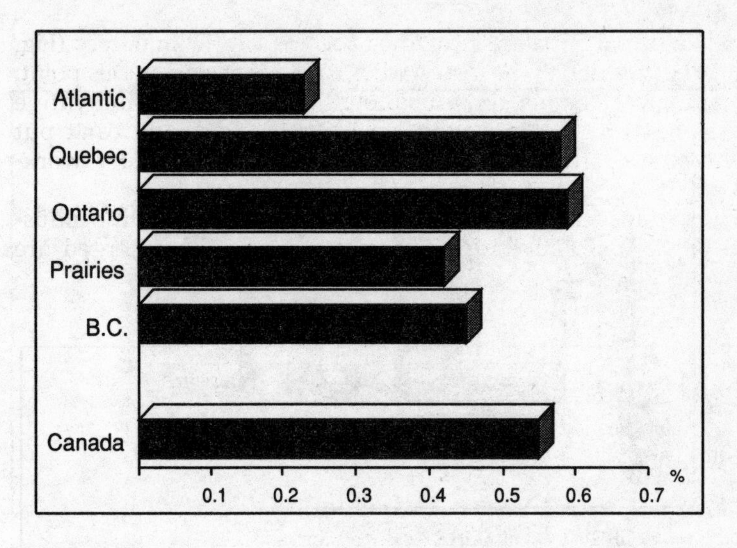

Figure 10.10 Expenditure on computer equipment as a proportion of sales by regions, 1980-5

Regional aspects

Not unexpectedly, in so vast a country, regional disparities abound in Canada. The Economic Council's survey results show that the regions of the industrial heartland (Quebec and Ontario) spent proportionately more on computer equipment than did the Atlantic provinces, the Prairies or British Columbia (Fig. 10.10).

Science and technology policy in Canada, including, specifically, the establishment of certain targets for R & D expenditure as a proportion of GNP, is a key element in regional and industrial strategy. Canada's heavy resource dependence, especially in the western and eastern provinces, is a source of considerable economic risk in a global environment characterised by badly depressed prices for primary commodities. Technology policy is a means to increased diversification.

Paradoxically, while the resource-dependent provinces have recognised this need, progress has been slow. The province of Ontario has itself a target for R & D expenditures of 2.5 per cent of GDP, but the Canadian ratio stood at 1.35 per cent in 1986 and has declined in real terms in recent years.

Only very recently has sufficient political will begun to emerge in Canada to establish the public policy framework within which

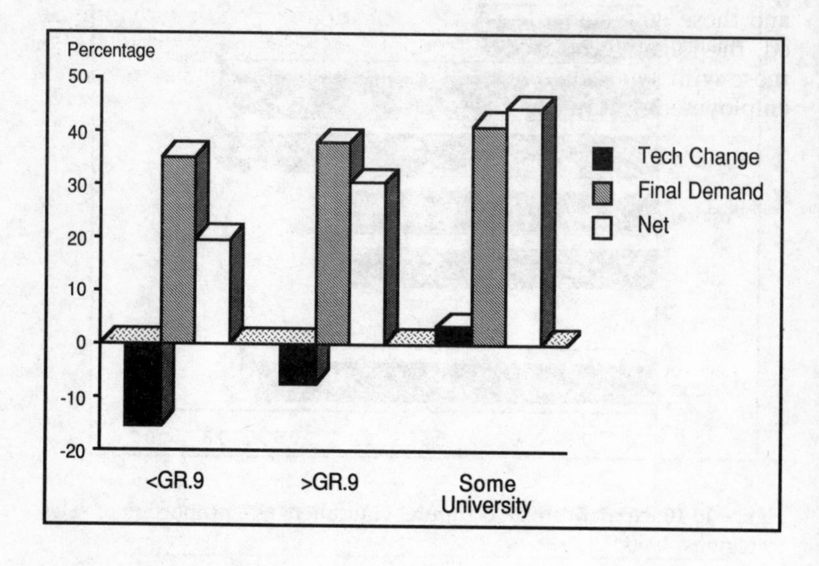

Figure 10.11 Change in employment due to changes in technology and final demand in three educational attainment groups, 1971-81

an articulated regional technology policy may be erected. A welcome step has been the establishment of the federal-provincial Council of Science and Technology Ministers which may, at least in principle, have the means to formulate a co-ordinated regional approach.

Concluding comments

One major conclusion emerges that is critical both for industrial regions and for the economy as a whole: the successful implementation of information technologies depends critically upon the preparation of a highly-skilled, flexible and versatile workforce that is assured of the opportunity to share equitably in the benefits of technological change. Education and human resources policies must go hand in hand with adoption of IT.

The importance of education is illustrated by Fig. 10.11, which shows the sources of employment change for three groups of workers ranked by educational attainment: those with less than grade 9 education, those with more than grade 9 but no university, and those with some university education. For the poorly educated, the negative impact of technological change is greatest. For those with some university education the technological impact on employment was actual positive.

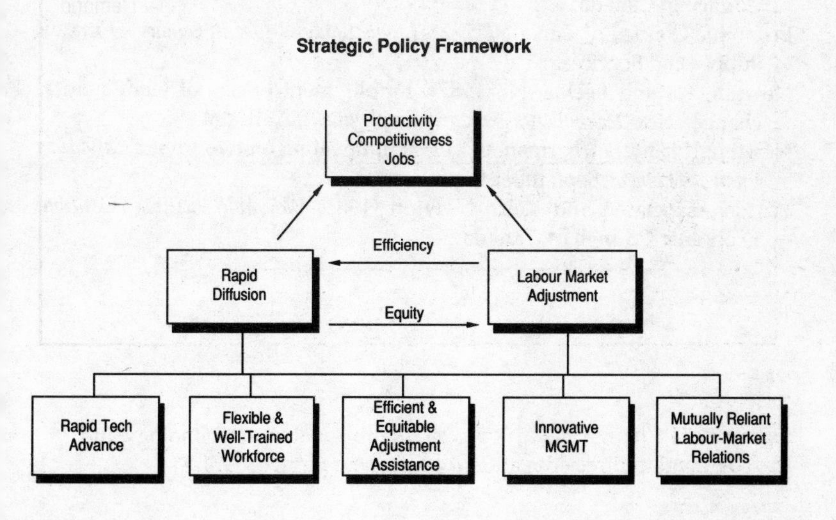

Figure 10.12 Strategic policy framework

Finally, the potential synergy between rapid technological diffusion and innovative human resources policies is suggested in Fig. 10.12, which shows that, in this instance, the goals of efficiency and equity may be pursued simultaneously.

Note:

This paper is based on research undertaken for the Economic Council of Canada. More detailed results are found in the Council's recent publications *Making Technology Work*, and *Innovation and Jobs in Canada*.

References

Betcherman, G. and McMullen, K. (1986)*Working with Technology: A Survey of Automation in Canada*. Ottawa: Economic Council of Canada.

McCurdy, T. (1988) *Employment, Income and Occupation Effects of Computer-Based Automation in Canada.* Discussion Paper No. 340. Ottawa: Economic Council of Canada.

Economic Council of Canada (1987). *Innovation and Jobs in Canada* . Ottawa: Supply and Services.

Newton, K., and Leckie, N. (1987) 'Employment effects of technological change.' *New Technology, Work and Employment*, Autumn.

Newton, K., and Betcherman, G. (1987) 'Innovating on two fronts.'*Canadian Business Review*, September.

Words Associated and Keith Newton (1986) *Workable Futures. Ottawa:* Economic Council of Canada.

11. Promotion of a regional information economy: the role of government and public sector institutions in partnership with industry

Walter Zegveld

Managing Director
TNO Division of Policy Research and Information
Delft, the Netherlands

Traditionally, regional industrial policy has focused primarily on offering various planning, property and financial incentives to firms to locate branch manufacturing plants in the so-called development regions as well as offering assistance to ailing (usually traditional) industries already located in these regions. Since the onset of the current period of industrial transformation, however, few firms appear to be seeking new decentralised locations. Strategy increasingly appears to be one of rationalisation and retrenchment, with many branch manufacturing plants being reduced in size, merged or closed down completely. Studies have shown that in most countries the encouragement of branch manufacturing plants has been disappointing as a means of increasing local levels of technological sophistication. These studies have pointed to lower levels of technical sophistication found in new regional branch plants when compared with their parent companies.

Because traditional regional economic policy has tended to be less effective during periods of economic stagnation and in the light of a technology related interpretation of long-term economic development, the question can be posed whether the time is ripe for a different approach to regional economic policy.

Whereas traditional regional policy places emphasis on the attraction of a propulsive unit - a growth pole - to regional development (an exogeneous strategy), it is now generally believed that a new regional policy should start with the existing potential of a region (an endogeneous strategy) and should to a large extent be based on increasing the potential of small and medium-sized firms in the region.

In some sectors small firms have considerable innovation potential. The technological performance of these firms is, however, to a large extent dependent on the technological requirements of local markets to which small firms, especially new firms, can be strongly bound. Lack of external communication with sources of scientific and technological knowledge, as well as with geographically distant and more advanced markets, can be a major disadvantage to smaller firms.

Because of the problems of external communication and as a result of the mostly traditional nature of small firm demand, three important elements of a new regional policy should be:

1. Improvement of small firms' access to sources of scientific, technological and other expertise.
2. Improvement in the quality of smaller firms' demand.
3. Better access to a wide range of government measures to stimulate innovation in industry.

Before going into the specifics of small-firm-oriented regional innovation policy, I will describe a number of more general issues in science and technology:

1. The increasing role of industry in R & D and in education and the change in industry-university relations..
2. The concentration on core business by large enterprises leading to increases in subcontracting and co-makership.
3. Regionalisation of research systems.

The increasing role of industry in R & D and in education

Scientific knowledge is increasingly recognised to be needed in a growing range of technological and economic activities which are, in turn, critical for growth, employment and international competitiveness. The demand for scientific knowledge is creating fundamental changes in the research and related higher education system. Two main directions of change are especially prominent:

1. The expanding efforts of firms to meet their internal needs for knowledge and education: the 'industrialisation' of R & D and education.
2. The marketing by academic institutions and other government subsidised institutions of research and educational services to business.

The 'Industrialisation' of research and education

The business sector is rapidly expanding its spending on research. From a quantitive standpoint nearly 100 per cent of the increase in national spending on R & D in the advanced economies over the period since 1980, amounting to between 0.5 and 0.7 per cent of GNP, took place in industry. In most industrialised countries the volume of R & D in industry has over the period increased by 50-70 per cent. The most pronounced case is Sweden. Whereas traditional spending on R & D in that country presently amounts to some 3 per cent of GNP, two-thirds of this volume is spent and paid for by industry. From a qualitative standpoint, the business sector in the USA and Japan has also increased its share of national spending for basic research. In the USA, business enterprise was responsible for 17 per cent of the total expenditure for basic research in 1986. Expenditures on basic research in Japan constitute 35 per cent of the country's total basic research spending. Both in Japan and the USA the absolute amount has doubled since 1980.

Spending by the business sector on basic research is concentrated in those industries involved in the development of new technologies: microelectronics, biotechnology and new materials. Industries involved in the new technologies, and operating in the international market, have little recourse but to direct more resources to research. Industrial laboratories often have a much larger critical mass of researchers in areas such as biotechnology, artificial intelligence and solid-state physics than individual academic institutions can possibly assemble. Furthermore, firms can more often afford more advanced research facilities. In addition to the efforts of individual firms, companies in a number of countries are forming research consortia, pooling resources to conduct research. In the USA, anti-trust legislation was lifted for that purpose. In a number of cases academic institutions participate in such consortia. Companies are also expanding their capabilities and involvement in research through numerous, often international, collaborative arrangements.

The pooling of research resources and the co-ordination of efforts on an international scale leads to an expansion of the kind and range of research which can be undertaken by individual firms and, thus, increases the extent to which research as a whole is becoming industrialised.

The clearest expression of market-led education exists in the USA. According to a report of the Carnegie Foundation titled 'Corporate classrooms' (1985) industry now spends about US$80 billion annually on educating their staff. Several firms have formal state accredited degree courses up to and including the PhD level and contract out specialised training needs to academics cooperating with them. In a number of European countries developments of these types are also taking place. In the Netherlands re-education and training by industry is estimated at $2 billion annually with an annual growth rate of 15-20 per cent.

From a standpoint of the provision of innovation supporting services to small and medium-sized firms, public institutions who have played a key role in this respect in the past will undoubtedly see their role and scope affected by the trend towards industrialisation of research and education.

The marketing by academic institutions of research and educational services to business

An OECD report of 1982 'The university and the community; the problem of changing relationships' noted that 'the university has lost a large part of its monopoly of higher education; research is increasingly being performed by specialised institutions or laboratories of large firms; the university is still not clear how it should bring separate disciplines together to study the great problems of our societies.' These trends have accelerated in many countries with respect to both research and education. Universities have greatly expanded, however, their marketing and commercial roles showing the increasing economic value of scientific knowledge. Universities have been forced to go this way because of constrained public funding but are experiencing limititations on access to research results in the process. How industrialisation of university research and internationalisation go together may be illustrated by the fact that presently the volume of contract research on behalf of Japanese firms by US universities is larger than that performed by Japanese universities.

The research often most pertinent to industrial needs is of a multidisciplinary nature. Few universities have succeeded in developing research of this kind. Research organisations outside of the university system, both public and private, seem to be more successful in this respect.

Extensive investment in human capital is now seen as essential for competitiveness of industry as well as for countries. To meet this demand, various universities are marketing education and training services. In an address to the US National Congress on Engineering Education (1986), R. W. Schmidt commented with respect to engineering education that too much separates students from the real world and prepares them for 'a culture of research and analysis rather than the competitive culture of industry'. A number of attempts are being made - especially in the USA through NSF initiatives - to redress this situation. Participation by universities in industry induced education programmes would also be a good mechanism to help align the regular university system to adjust to present needs. It would be appropriate to consider access to such specially designed industrialised education on behalf of small and medium-sized firms as well. These firms too need well trained personnel and usually are too small to organise fruitful relationships with universities for these purposes themselves.

Flexibility-induced concentration on core-business by large enterprises leading to increase in subcontracting and co-makership

The most explicit policy formulations indicating the role and organisation of government to foster small and medium-sized firms can be found in the USA and in Japan. Both countries have formulated comprehensive legislation to this effect. In the USA, this legislation has taken the form of a Small Business Act, dating back to 1953. In Japan similar legislation, in the form of the Fundamental Law of Small-Medium Enterprises was passed in 1963. In Japan the Small Business Co-operation along with 160 different institutions at national and regional levels ensures that SMEs do not suffer diseconomies of scale by promoting sharing of resources through joint factory complexes, shared transport centres and sales outlets, co-operative computer and CAD/CAM centres, co-operative management training centres and testing facilities. Similarly, mechanisms of this kind have worked extremely well in fostering SME development in other countries. The example of Japan has been presented for the purpose of showing a structural set-up in a large industrial society for advancing SMEs. Under the Small Business Legislation in both the USA and Japan, there are rules for subcontracting to SMEs in the case of government procurement contracts to larger firms.

In an effort to increase its flexibility, there is at present a more general movement by large industry towards subcontracting and co-makership. Although the extent of such movement is difficult to grasp, many large firms in Europe are reported to be following this route of decentralisation. For the large firm this movement means flexibility, for the SME it often means contact with a technologically advanced and knowledgeable client.

Several European firms are reported to transfer substantial knowledge to their subcontractors in an effort to make them meet their specifications and subjects cited in this respect are production technology, quality assurance, logistics and so on. Provided that the dependence of SMEs on single clients does not become too large, this phenomena could well prove an excellent manner of transfer of knowledge through the provision of the advanced markets that large firms provide.

Regionalisation of research systems

Competition between regions to attract knowledge-oriented organisations is often quite severe. A manifestation of regionalisation - and often of competition between regions - is the increase in the number of science parks. After a first small wave of such parks occurring some fifteen to twenty years ago, a second round appeared in the early 1980s. The second-wave parks, typically, are mainly developed through partnerships of an academic institution, a regional authority and a financial institution. While the form and nature of science parks vary considerably, the current listing is impressive:

1. In the USA there are an estimated 150 science and research parks with an equal number expected to be created within the next ten years.
2. In Japan, the Technopolis programme involves twenty-five academic institutions in its main parklike effort.
3. In Europe there are at present more than fifty university centred parks in operation and several times this number without formal academic links. Many more are being envisaged or are in the planning stage.

There are, in addition, various other kinds of local initiatives which are acting to regionalise research, training and employment of scientists and engineers. The aim is to promote a continuous circle of relationships, leading to contact, understanding, communication, mutual reward and further contact, which leads to enduring and evolving collaboration.

Present public policy towards small and medium-sized enterprises (SMEs)

For the purpose of present policy, SMEs can be divided into three broad categories: SMEs in traditional industries; modern niche-strategy SMEs; and new-technology-based firms.

SMEs in traditional industries

These are firms operating in areas such as textiles, footwear, woodworking. Often they will have been established for many years. They will increasingly be facing competition from low labour-cost countries. They need access mainly to existing technology to upgrade the quality of the products they produce, to improve the efficiency of their production process and to update design. Microelectronics can offer them many opportunities both in quality control and improvement in productivity. Such firms also often need access to managment expertise; how to control and organise the production sequence better; better purchasing and stock control procedures, and so on. Various schemes are being offered in several European countries combining both technical and managerial aspects which together fulfil the requirements of SMEs rather well in this category.

Modern niche-strategy SMEs

These are typically companies in the scientific instruments, electronic subsystem, specialist machinery and equipment areas and in the CAD industry. They use up-to-date technology to supply often custom-built products to special market niches. Their needs are mainly access to R & D expertise, access to funds for major new developments, assistance with patenting and access to markets.

New-technology-based firms

NTBFs are in a special class and play an important role in the diffusion of new technologies, at least in the USA. Important factors in the formation and rapid growth of NTBFs are:

1. A cultural climate favouring entrepreneurship.
2. Access to state-of-the-art technology.
3. The ability to spin-off from centres of state-of-the-art expertise, mainly firms and universities.
4. Availability of venture capital and the provision of temporary and part-time management support.
5. The presence of risk-accepting markets.

Of course, no single one of these measures will be sufficient. It is necessary to implement a coherent set of measures both on the supply side and the demand side.

Characteristics of an effective system of technology transfer

An approach aimed at elevating the level of competence of SMEs has been successfully employed in a number of countries and for a number of decades in the agricultural sector. This system comprises a collective research infrastructure supported through a network of transfer points to the agricultural sector. Although it is important to note at the outset that because of strong differences in market conditions, industrial sectors cannot be fully compared with the agricultural sector, the latter can provide useful pointers to some of the basic elements required for success in the transfer of knowledge.

In the USA a great many attempts have in fact been undertaken to apply the agricultural extension model to other sectors by providing education, development aid and the dissemination of technical knowledge to industrial firms. None of these attempts has, however, been successful. Rogers *et al.* (1976) have analysed the reason for these failures and have come up with eight main characteristics with which an effective knowledge transfer system has to comply:

1. The system has to have at its disposal a critical quantity of new knowledge. The quality and level of research, together with information from international sources, represent a major source of new information of potential value to the user.
2. Part of the system must be oriented towards application and implementation. Most of the researchers and the extension personnel must have a strong orientation towards practice. An important factor in the agricultural sector is that researchers and extension personnel often have an agricultural background.
3. Users of research results must have a substantial influence on the research and information services.
4. Structural mechanisms must exist between the different components of the overall system, namely between fundamental research, applied research and the extension services.
5. Contacts between the information service agent and the user must be frequent.
6. The social distance between suppliers and users of information must be bridged.
7. Research, information services and education must be treated as a single system.
8. The system must have an important influence on the environment. This influence must be shown in political and economic power and in the legitimacy of the system.

The value of the model presented by Rogers lies in the philosophy behind it. Hence, the agricultural sector does offer an important model for (re)thinking the process of development, transfer and application of knowledge to SMEs at the regional level.

Towards a future concept of regional innovation supporting services

The developments described earlier in this paper, industrialisation of research and education, flexibility induced concentration on core-business by large firms and the regionalisation of research systems, are very likely to alter the more traditional concept of regional SME supporting services. Furthermore, SMEs are of different categories and each category needs a different kind of support. Characteristics of an effective system of technology transfer have been put forward against which new policies have to be checked.

In putting forward an overall concept of regional innovation supporting services, it is important to put such a new concept in the context of national innovation policy. National innovational policies vary from country to country and attention should be given to the main characteristics of such policy.

It is apparent that in an approach towards the structural transformation of industry into higher added value, more knowledge-intensive sectors and product groups, and the creation of major technology-based industries serving new markets, science and technology are necessary - although not sufficient - elements. As part of innovation policy, governments have initiated so-called national technology programmes. Examples of such programmes include NASA's development of satellite communications in the USA, the Alvey programme for advanced information technology in the UK (and its several national and international counterparts), the offshore equipment programme in Norway, the development of agricultural technology in the Netherlands and the pharmaceutical industry in Sweden. These approaches have in common that linkage or integrating mechanisms are provided: linking publicly funded and/or infrastructurally performed R & D to industrial companies, linking together different industrial firms, linking private and public sector interests and in a number of cases linking research with education. It can be stated that large firms are the most closely affected by such policies because of the orientation of the programmes as well as the general inability of SMEs to participate, thresholds often being too high for smaller firms.

With respect to small and medium-sized enterprises I have given a divison in three broad categories, namely SMEs in traditional industries, modern niche-strategy SMEs, and new-technology-based firms. A whole range of measures has been devised in all countries to assist these firms in their innovative endeavours. It can be concluded that although the large number of such measures most probably reflects serious attempts by policy-makers to advance the innovative potential and practice of SMEs, the effects of such measures are very difficult to evaluate and their success is generally not considered large. Given their large number, relatively few SMEs have taken advantage of these measures. This has been caused by a number of factors, including the lack of awareness on the side of SMEs and the inability to bridge the gap between policy-makers and their potential clients. At the start of this chapter I have pointed to the need for changes in regional policy. A new approach in supporting SMEs on the basis of regional innovation supporting services would now be to focus on the development of the institutional framework of such services. One of the principal features of this approach is a stricter regionalisation: a substantially large number of regions or districts as compared with the earlier days of regional policy. Another basic feature is a voluntary co-operation between regional industry at large, regional authorities, banks, research institutions and educational institutions, including universities: a public - private partnership in the scientific technological and educational infrastructure.

The aim of such an approach is a partnership among local economic and social actors with sufficient local private or public knowledge, know-how and means to offer to SMEs in a low-threshold manner. Also to be provided by this network are links and directions to sources of knowledge outside the region. This approach entails not only active and co-ordinated participation of all relevant local actors, but would need a local agent, to be seen as representing the local interest, to put the network together. This approach or concept would be a more present-day type of regional innovation policy. It is of strategic value in that it pursues a long-range improvement of the position of the district. It draws together the most interesting aspects of industrial sector innovation, policies for small firms, and for regional development. It is an optimal setting for providing tailor-made solutions for local needs, and truly actively combines the district's endogenous potential.

Although the number of examples of such new concepts of regional innovation supporting services is still small, Italian experience is particularly interesting (Mazzonis and Pianta 1987). Parallels have been reported in French regional policy and in policies pursued by a number of US states - including Michigan - and some large US cities. Also regional approaches in Denmark, the UK and Baden Württemburg and Finland would come close to the above concept. The activities in the Netherlands of INDUMA at Helmond and REEDE at Eindhoven; providing access for SMEs to Philips' knowledge (including subcontracting) are further examples.

The Advisory Committee on Technology Policy in the Netherlands under the chairmanship of Dr W. Dekker, former president of Philips, recently proposed, among other things, the establishment of a relatively large number (twenty) of regional Innovation Advisory Centres (IACs) close to SMEs (Dekker 1987). It has been proposed that these IACs play a role both on behalf of individual firms and groups of firms and that they would also act as an executive agent for some of the national measures. As such, these IACs very well fit the overall concept of regional innovation supporting services.

Areas of activity of the IACs are many. They depend on the structure of local industry and on the preparedness of the local actors concerned to cooperate. Among the areas are:

the creation of awareness
re-education and training
technology monitoring
logistics
marketing
quality control
energy saving

environmental control
subcontracting and co-makership
technological counselling and
general management

Also to be included are the relationships with other national and international schemes.

It is a widely held view internationally that the persons organising these new regional networks should act as facilitators not doers; catalysers not controllers; influencers not imposers. They should organise resources for functions which could be shared by various SMEs and if necessary large organisations too; and ensure critical mass for a great many multifaceted regional requirements.

It should not be overlooked that both requirements and potential for functions to be organised differ from region to region, and that the way in which regions would reorganise for executing these functions will show substantial differences as well. Involvement of central government in these local activities (e.g. in co-financing) will have to take such diversity into account.

The core of the concept is to innovate regional schemes for SMEs in such a way that they really work to the benefit of this category of firm. The concept involves both public and private actors and is largely based on responsibility being taken from within the region. Next to producer services of government it also includes producer services of private organisations.

References

Carnegie Foundation (1985) *Corporate Classrooms: The Learning Business*.

Dekker, W. (Chairman) (1987) *Report of the Committee on the Extension of Technology Policy in the Netherlands*. The Hague, April.

Mazzonis, D., and Pianta, M. (1987) 'A new approach to innovation in traditional industries: the experience of ENEA in the Italian context.' Paper prepared for the UN-CSTD panel on technology promotion polices for SMEs. Guangzhou China, November.

OECD. (1987) 'Science and technology policy outlook - 1987'. Draft paper, June.

Rogers, E. M., Eveland, J. P., and Bean, A. S. (1976). *Extending the Agricultural Extension Model*. Stanford, Calif: Stanford University, Institute for Communication Research.

Rothwell, R., and Zegveld, W. (1981). *Industrial Innovation and Public Policy*. London: Frances Pinter.

(1982) *Innovation and the Small and Medium-Sized Firm*. London: Frances

Pinter.
(1985) *Reindustrialisation and Technology.* London: Longman.
Zegveld, W. (1987) 'Small and medium firms and technology policy in the Netherlands.' Paper prepared for the UN-CSTD panel on technology promotion policies for SMEs. China, Guangzhou, November.
Zegveld, W., and Enzing, C. (1986) *New Issues in Science and Technology Policy.* Report prepared for the Directorate General for Science Policy, Netherlands Ministry of Education and Science. Delft.

12. Information systems for networks of small and medium-sized enterprises: ENEA's experience

Agostino Mathis

Director for Information Systems, ENEA, Rome

For many years now the Nuclear and Alternative Energy Agency (ENEA) has been active in the promotion of innovation in manufacturing industry, devoting special attention to the needs of small and medium-sized enterprises (SMEs). This activity was part of the agency's mandate for the upgrading of Italian industry's energy technology. More recently the agency has been specifically called upon by government and Parliament to generate innovation by means of the transfer of advanced technologies to the whole Italian production system, but especially to SMEs.

The introduction of any kind of new technology nowadays, and that includes technologies concerned with optimum utilisation of energy sources, cannot be carried out from a single-sector viewpoint: it has increasingly to take into account all the various aspects of current, or possible, organisational changes in the situation under consideration. Consequently, it should be quite clear that the problems connected with the introduction of efficient information systems, in support of all the management and operation processes inherent in such situations, are rapidly gaining in importance.

An intellectual technology

The innovatory scope of traditional technologies (the mechanical, electrotechnical, thermotechnical ones, etc.) was usually completely built into the machines designed to do the specific job - and they called for relatively limited and rapidly achievable training for the workers concerned.

On the other side, as all of us now know, the new information technologies involve the end-users' intellectual ability and their socio-organisation structures in a critical way. The information system (whether it be hardware, software or a combination of the two) is, in itself, a semi-finished product, while the overall efficiency of the utilisation of information systems is essentially dependent on the preparation of the socio-organisational structures in general and on the specific entrepreneurial and professional skills of the individual end-users. Such a situation leads one to maintain that new information technologies are qualitatively different from previous technologies and, as such, they can be looked upon as 'intellectual technologies' (Pyburn and Curley 1984).

These considerations take on fundamental importance if the new information technologies are to be used as strategic instruments for the extension and diversification of companies' activities, rather than just as substitutes for out-of-date technologies or manpower in the same production processes.

In the light of this novel way of looking at things, we have the concept of 'software' which breaks out of the more strictly technical definition (a collection of rules and procedures that inform machines how to do their jobs) to take on the meaning of global systematisation which includes not just the technical aspects but also and above all those concerned with organisation and training in the whole company situation. Looked at this way, activity concerned with software becomes a continuous creative process which involves the evolution of company strategies, innovation in company organisation and, specially, continuous training of company human resources which without any doubt is regarded today as the critical factor in any company's success (*Media Duemila* 1987).

Even though technological development is usually looked upon from the general public's point of view as a means for creating highly sophisticated devices such as robots or space weapons, the fact is that the essential premises for any social structure achieving maturity (including a technological one), lies in organisational know-how - in other words, organisational software. We are still dealing, if you like, with a technology, but it is an abstract and invisible one which the majority of people do not even notice; it does, however, constitute the motive force for the development of any organisation - be it industrial or social.

The know-how comprises not only the programs that tell the computers what to do, and written procedures for factory and office but a large part of the know-how also gets stored in the minds of individual human beings - just one more confirmation of the increasingly critical nature of the human contribution in a period in which technology seemed to be taking over.

Certain historical examples can be cited in favour of this analysis of the situation. The efficiency of Scandinavian Public Administration organisations, for some time now based on an optimum use of information technologies, did not so much grow out of a specially original Scandinavian skill in the development of microelectronics or computer infrastructures. It grew from the fact that research and teaching centres, specifically aimed at planning those new organisational structures best able to make use of the information technologies, have been operative for decades, at all levels from the academic downwards. One can cite as an example Professor Langefors' school at Stockholm University and the methodology that came out of it, based on analysis of change, first from an organisational standpoint and then from a technological one.

In the same way the success of the Japanese industrial system in recent decades was not, at the beginning, so much based on original technological developments, as on a systematic rethink of traditional production processes in the light of their own cultural reality and the evolution of world markets.

Structural change

In Italy, after the social and structural crises of the 1970s, the major national companies - at least those that still had some life in them - have managed to update themselves radically, sometimes arriving at organisational solutions that are truly original in a global sense. In the case of these major enterprises the role of the public administration must essentially be aimed at preserving and improving the environment in which these enterprises operate. It would be difficult for the public administration to intervene in an efficient and timely way in the definition of future policies for technical and organisational evolutions.

The situation, however, is quite different with regard to SMEs (and from an operative point of view artisan and craft organisations must certainly be included here as well). In this sector, as well, it is widely recognised that in the last ten years Italy has shown the world some unique examples of vitality and innovative ability, by means of a sort of grafting of industrial entrepreneurship into situations with ancient municipal, mercantile and craft traditions. It can in fact be said that the maintenance of acceptable economic conditions in Italy at the end of the 1970s, when the major enterprises were going through their worst period, was largely thanks to that unforeseen development of spontaneous and widespread entrepreneurship.

The restructuring of major organisations was very often brought about by the deverticalisation of the production processes and their decentralisation in small outside enterprises often widely scattered throughout the country. By so doing a considerable degree of flexibility and quick reaction to the demands of an evolving market was achieved. With few exceptions, however, the vast majority of SMEs and artisan and craft organisations were practically excluded from these organisational and managerial criteria. As has been already suggested, some of the advantages of these types of enterprises (such as swift and flexible reactions to market demands, decentralisation of decision making, low indirect costs) tend to disappear rapidly as a consequence of the introduction of the new information technologies in the major concerns and in organically structured inter-company systems.

These larger structures, because they can usually count on a much higher level of entrepreneurship and of financial and technological resources, inevitably have a tendency towards attaining unreachable strategic supremacy in the main sectors of production.

It is quite clear, then, what challenge faces SMEs and craft industries in the coming years. They have to define and implement organisational, professional and technological changes so as to put themselves into the position of being able to compete efficiently, at least in certain sectors, with the major industrial groups.

Clearly, in a scenario of this sort, there is ample room for public bodies able to promote correctly the technical and organisational changes in the area of small` and medium-sized enterprises.

Prato and the SPRINT project

ENEA is already the author of a large number of interventions for the development of information systems for networks of SMEs. The first of these, and the one which is today the most developed, is without doubt the Telematics Project for the Prato area. The Prato area is one of the largest concentrations of textile manufacturing in Italy, and in the world. There are more than 10,000 enterprises, mainly of an artisan or craft nature. The workforce has reached the figure of 70,000 and the annual sales can be put at US$ 5 billion. In Table 12.1 the most important socio-economic aspects of the Prato area are outlined.

The innovative programme for the Prato textile zone, which includes the Telematics Project, has as its protagonist the SPRINT Association ('Sistema Prato Innovazione Technologica'). The origin of the Association can be traced to a proposal made by ENEA. The three founder members of the SPRINT Association - UIP (the Union of Prato Industrialists), AMAP (the Prato section of the Confederation of Artisans) and CNA (the Prato section of the National Confederation of Artisans and Craftsmen), as well as ENEA of course, were joined by a whole series of other organisations - STET (the telephone company), the Florence Chamber of Commerce, Cassa di Risparmi e Depositi di Prato (CRP, the Savings and Deposit Bank of Prato), the Municipality of Prato, the Monte di

Paschi di Siena bank, the Banca Popolare di Novara, the Istituto Bancario San Paolo di Torino bank, the Banca Toscana, the Cassa di Risparmio di Pistoia e Pescia (savings bank) and the Prato section of the Unified Textile Workers' Trade Union (FULTA). The finance supply to SPRINT, apart from many of the Association members and principally ENEA, the Cassa di Risparmi e Depositi di Prato (CRP) and the Florence Chamber of Commerce, comes from the Tuscan regional government and the EEC.

Table 12.1 Economic data concerning the textile area (estimates)

Statistical data

- The Prato textile area: Prato, Agliana,Barberino, Calenzano, Campi Bisenzio, Cantagallo, Carmignano, Montale, Montemurlo, Poggio a Caiano, Quarrata,Vaiano, Vernio
- Population: 300,000
- Manufacturing Industry: 22,000 local manufacturing units
- Manufacturing Industry: 94,000 employees
- Textile Industry: 15,000 local textile manufacturing units, of which 2,000 of an industrial nature
- Textile Industry: 66,000 employees
- Woollen Industry: 10,000 local manufacturing units
- Woollen Industry: 42,000 employees
- Textile Industry Turnover: Lire 5,000 billion
- Textile Industry Exports: Lire 2,500 billion

Production potential

- 800,000 spindles of carded wool material (70% of Italy's total)
- 400,000 spindles of wool top (15% of Italy's total)
- 15,000 looms (50% of the Italian woollen sector)

Destination of the production by market segment

- Haute couture; top-class ready-made clothes	14%
- Boutiques; specialised large stores	50%
- Mass consumption	36%

The objective of the Telematics Project was the creation of an information system in support of the Prato area's textile production system, based on a telematic network using videotex technology. Starting from the results of research into information flows between operators in the Prato area, co-ordinated by the Milanese company RESEAU srl, in 1985 a technical committee, limited to those members of the SPRINT Association that were effectively interested in the utilisation of the network, carried out a detailed analysis of the information systems being used and the communication and information needs that were not being met. The result was the definition of the contents and specifications for a packet of services to be put into action in the experimental stage.

In 1986 the technical and operational aspects of the network were defined. It had to be compatible at lowest costs, with the information technology realities of the existing suppliers of services. This implied the active involvement of the people in charge of the SPRINT partners' data processing centres which were candidates for becoming 'information suppliers' for the area's information system. These were people who had nearly always been operating under difficult conditions as far as EDP resources and personnel were concerned, and they were called upon to accept major modifications to their way of looking at EDP services, to accept a double operational system for the services that they had previously supplied by traditional means and - even more exacting - to take a deep new look at their centre's development strategies. The centre created at Prato became the interface between local data processing centres and the nation-wide Videotel system run by SIP, the Italian state-owned telephone company.

A special agreement was drawn up between SPRINT and SIP aimed at guaranteeing the efficiency and reliability of the whole Prato area communications network and the Videotel service, at speeding up existing plans for digitising the area's network, at making it possible to interconnect with ITAPAC and RFD special networks, and at bringing Prato into the integrated-service digital network pilot scheme.

The signing of this agreement marked the end of the planning phase of the Telematics Project and the beginning of its realisation, with the direct involvement of the 'information supplier' partners (the FI). The activities of the FI were defined, assisted and rendered compatible centrally by SPRINT, which entrusted the co-ordination task to the above mentioned RESEAU srl and the technical direction to ENEA. Both of these organisations were further charged with technical and economical evaluation, financial management and administration of all the hardware, software, telecommunications and human resources involved in the project.

All the components of the project - the data processing structures of the SPRINT centre and the centres of the individual FI, the services, the users, the experimental task-force,and so on - were available by November 1987, and at the beginning of 1988 the experimental period became operative with about 250 sample users' terminals installed.

It must be emphasised that activities aimed at involving the users themselves in a favourable climate, where the proposed solutions can be assessed in tranquillity, are aspects of primary importance in the success of a complex project such as the Prato Telematics one - which, among other things, has the aim of verifying, at system level, the efficiency of solutions involving highly innovative methodologies. With this in mind, a scheme was drawn up for the sample users as well as for the staff of the associations involved in the operation of the services and in contacts with the users: the scheme was designed to make them aware of the issues involved and to give them specific training in the new approach. In support of this scheme a training course has been implemented for a specific 'task-force' of about twenty young people, aided by public grants; they will also be used during the course of 1988 to monitor the system when the experimental phase becomes operational.

The initial decision to create an area's telematic infrastructure which was undertaken after favourable technical and economical evaluation - bearing in mind also the non-compatibility of the existing information installations - in fact created an opportunity to get constructive collaboration on concrete initiatives going between all those operating in the area; it also created an opportunity for the dissemination at all levels of the first elements of a professionality open to the new information technologies.

For the best use to be made of this new infrastructure, especially as an innovative instrument for the implementation of new development strategies for the whole Prato 'area system', in parallel with the dissemination of telematic equipment, the time has now come to develop a reference planning scheme for the new information flows in the 'area system'. In the context of this planning scheme specifications and operative priorities can be gradually established for all the application procedures.

Prato's structure

To arrive at a better understanding of the role of information flows in a context such as the Prato textile area, a deeper study of the very particular characteristics of its transformation and management processes and their relative organisational structures should be undertaken.

The Prato textile system is often compared to a single large-scale industrial concern, and this analogy often gives rise to hurried judgements. In a context such as Prato, in fact, one must evaluate the effective existence and importance of management processes typical of large companies with unified and centralised management. In Fig. 12.1 a scheme of the Prato area system has been set out with special emphasis on the transformation and management processes. In Fig. 12.2 these processes are combined with organisational factors.The management processes are analysed with reference to the three levels into which company roles are usually classified - the general, the executive and the operational.

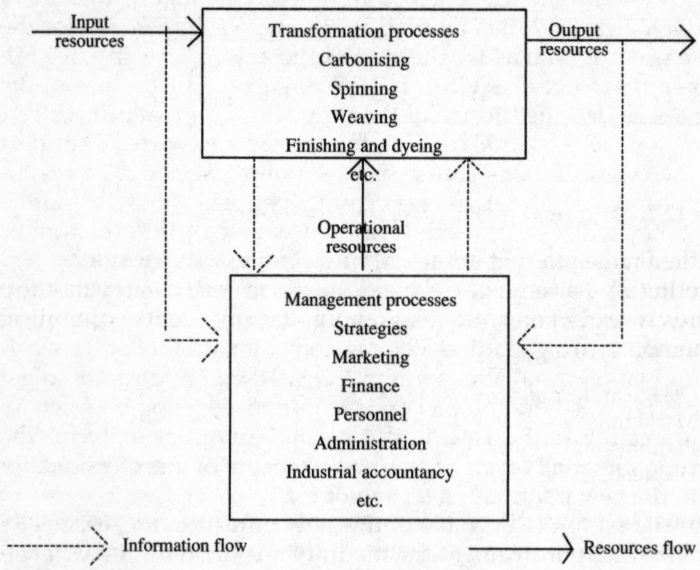

Figure 12.1. Prato area system: process schema.

At the general level, processes concerned with strategies, external relations (including marketing) and finance are not carried out by institutionalised departments with specific mandates. In essence they come about spontaneously, though they are often extremely effective and timely.

A single overall strategy based on quantitative data for the whole of the Prato textile context clearly does not exist. However there is a growing tendency towards the collection and utilisation of global data relative to the whole area and their analysis in common for possible future lines of development on the part of the major category Associations (the Industrialists' Association and the two Prato Craft Associations) as well as the Banks particularly the

Cassa di Risparmi e Depositi di Prato and the local Public Administration bodies.

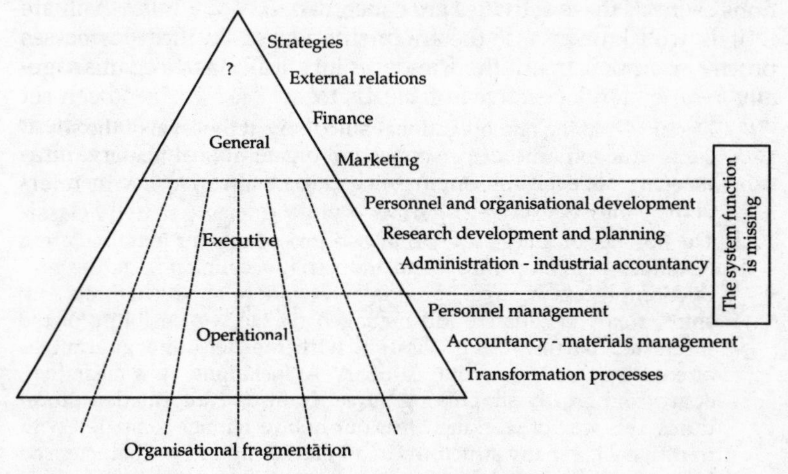

Figure 12.2. Prato area system: processes/organisation

In the Prato system it is widely know that external relations, and marketing in particular, are mainly carried out by impannatori (textile trade operators) - that is to say units operating autonomously which look after:

1. Design and promotion of new products.
2. Marketing.
3. Planning and control of orders for production.
4. Dispatch and invoicing.

It must be remembered that, apart from the few hundred textile trade operators in the strict sense of the word, some verticalised textile firms of medium size (woollen manufacturers) have a tendency to deal with these functions internally. As far as finance is concerned, business guidelines and value-added services tend to refer to the area's leading bank, which has already been mentioned.

As things stand at the moment, the 'Prato system'lacks the structural prerequisites for making full use of the opportunities offered by the new technological and organisational schemes which can make the systematic extension of company strategies possible for instance by means of the organic implementation of the commercial structures and the financial function. Well-known examples in Italy are Benetton in the ready-made clothes sector and Barilla in foodstuffs, and so on.

On the executive level typical company processes are concerned with personnel and organisational development, new product design, and the planning and control of production. The special characteristics of the Prato system have very important implications as far as these activities are concerned.

It is well known that the fragmentation of the transformation processes among many thousands of juridically and organisationally independent operative units leads to:

1. Decision-making and operational autonomy at the level of the smallest production unit for personnel and organisational matters: often there are not even any employees because the workers are members of the family or even working partners.
2. The absence of a need for formalised procedures for manufacturing resources planning (MRP) and industrial accountancy, as the production process is carried out via a network of contractual relationships, freely negotiated and managed on the responsibility of the interested parties, often, though, with the help and guarantees offered by their respective category Associations. It is clear that, apart from greatly simplifying bureaucratic and information procedures, this way of working turns out to be a winner compared with traditional company structures in all market situations characterised by marked and rapid variations in economic conditions and client preferences.
3. Finally, very widespread new product design closely linked with the external relations function. Between textile trade operators and medium to large industrial concerns, we are talking about hundreds of creative centres each producing sample collections and competing with the others (and with other national and international situations); it has however been possible to evaluate that the production of sample collections by traditional methods has reached costs of up to 10 per cent of turnover!

On the operational level the functions to be carried out are the well known ones of personnel management, accountancy (both industrial and fiscal), materials management and manufacturing (or, more generally, the transformation of flows of resources).

The decentralisation and the fragmentation of the decision-making and operational functions in the Prato system has obvious consequences also at this operational level:

1. For the reasons already mentioned, personnel management has become quantitatively simplified, but, wherever regularly employed workers are involved, all the legal and contractual norms (becoming more and more complicated and continuously being modified) have to be applied rigorously; this makes it very difficult for small operators to apply the regulations correctly and in proper time, and for some time now they have been induced to making use of outside services either private organisations or services provided by their category associations, with all the consequences that this gives rise to (manual data transfer, slowness in obtaining results, corrections to the results, costs).

2. Although they are always there, accountancy problems have become much simplified particularly after the recent evolution in fiscal regulations: the considerations made previously about personnel management substantially apply in this field as well.
3. Materials management is partly a consequence of the contractual nature of production planning, which by itself should lead to a natural minimisation of stocks, dead time and, hence, costs; it must however be said that, given the mainly casual location of the various operators in a far from rational urban context, and bearing in mind that another different operator category - the transporters - becomes involved,

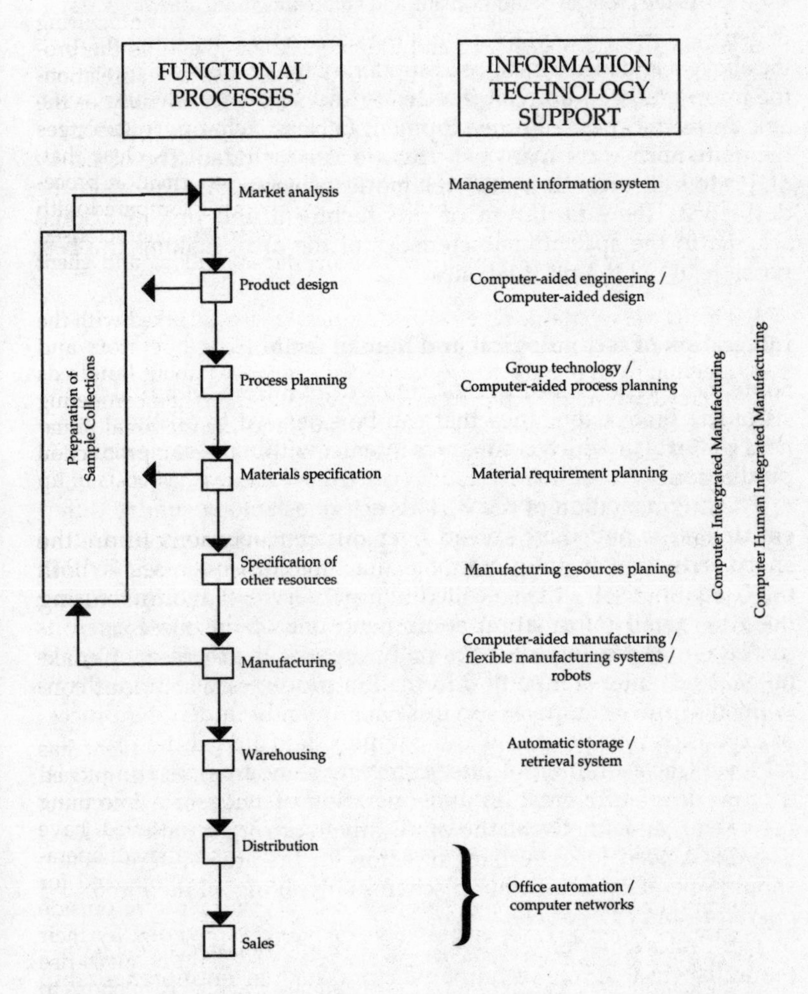

Figure 12.3 Integration of information technologies in manufacturing processes.

great potential improvements for these operations can be foreseen if information flows are reorganised and automated.

4. Finally, the transformation processes, which are firmly linked to current socio-organisational structures; in the past, as is well known, the main processes were based on small modular work centres (looms or groups of looms) which by their nature were suitable for undertakings with few employees (even family concerns); now that information technology and automation have made integration and co-ordinated optimisation possible for various phases of the production processes, it is difficult to justify their continued existence at different production units (consider the example of the problem of rationalising and automating the carding process).

In general terms Figure 12.3 sets out the schema for integrating many of the above mentioned functions in support of the production processes: the information equipment (hardware and software), already available or in the course of development (at least what is suitable for the more normal company set-ups) are also included. The objective of Prato's information and telematic projects can therefore be defined as the adaptation of this technical and organisational schema to the special characteristics of the area, making the best possible use of the positive ones.

Integration of technological and human factors

Some more general indications can be drawn from an initial analysis of the Prato experience that can be extended to all those business contexts in which companies interact within the same sector of production.

The fragmentation of the various activities among sundry different operators and their spread over different locations leads to a sharp reduction in intra-company information processes (within the company itself - the so-called internal services) and the relative need to install information equipment, one of the most onerous undertakings for large traditionally organised processes. On the other hand, inter-company information processes which might be defined as inter-company services consequently undergo a process of expansion and pose new and complex demands at the procedural level (the definition of inter-company standards), at the infrastructure level (the creation and operation of widescale telematic networks), and finally at the applicative and organisational level (there is a need for a systems function for the area-system, which should operate via association schemes involving all the interested operators and categories).

The Prato experience has spotlighted another decisive factor - the indispensable role of human factors, such as entrepreneurship and creativity - in every phase of the production process. It should be noted that it was this very role, which emerged during the decentralisation of production brought on by the 1947-55 post-war crisis, which made it possible for the Prato area-system to move progressively from a supply-oriented production system to a demand-oriented one, and hence the consequent shift from producing a few mass-market products to making a sophisticated range of high quality products, most of which were destined for the top of the fashion market.

In such a situation any installation of information and automation equipment could not but respect the driving force of the human factor in every phase of the process: from marketing to design, from weaving to finishing up. It therefore calls for an original organisation of the schemes for automation. Tools already partly available to the large manufacturing organisations have to be cleverly transferred and then carefully personalised. The aim should be not so much towards CIM (Computer Integrated Manufacturing) as to CHIM (Computer Human Integrated Manufacturing).

In this regard it should also be noted that even large vertically structured manufacturing concerns are experiencing increasing doubts about the advisability of going after completely computerised solutions, because of inherent limits to adaptability, reliability and availability.

The Prato experience, in its socio-organisational aspects, has shown how a high level of go-ahead entrepreneurship and traditional motivation towards innovation among the people involved are absolutely indispensable for the success of initiatives of this sort. The aim of outside intervention is therefore essentially to open up new prospects, to contribute knowledge and skills from other technological sectors, in the first instance to take the place of, and subsequently to develop in the local context, all the new organisational structures that are necessary for making the best use of the new information technologies.

As far as the Prato Telematics Project is concerned, a specially constituted company works at the local level on behalf of the SPRINT Association, which has also set up an in-house steering committee for telematics with a brief to define, plan and control the specific applications (individual user services, common data banks, etc.), and the training and diffusion programmes for the new technology. The SPRINT Association itself, through this type of structure, is thus taking on the germinal role of the new systems function with particular regard for its more strictly strategic and organisational tasks. It should be remembered that, besides ENEA and STET - the nation-wide technology organisations - all the interested parties in the area are members of SPRINT, Industrialists' and Craft

Associations, trade unions, the local administration, banks. These very members have stated that SPRINT's activity has by itself achieved results never before obtained in the history of the Prato area: the setting up of a system of relationships between all the interested parties to discuss, define and decide upon initiatives that, though originated by technological developments, will inevitably take on strategic importance over the next decades for the socio-economic evolution of the entire area.

The agency role

If we take these previously described experiences, and others more recently set in motion, it would seem possible to draw some conclusions for the systematic organisation of interventions of this type in the context of national programmes for the promotion of innovation in production activities.

Between technology and its adaptation to the socio-organisation context - the two necessary factors for innovation in production activities - it is to be noted that the former is increasingly becoming a variable which is external to the national situation. By now even applicative innovations, and not just basic innovations, have become factors that require an international dimension to be efficiently acquired and operated and in practice, multinational companies and inter-company agreements are needed for the dissemination and after-sales service of the new systems on the market.

On the other hand, the introduction of new technologies to special situations such as the majority of small and medium-sized Italian companies is a task that can be dealt with autonomously in these more limited dimensions. In any case its delegation would not seem to be possible.

The tradition of vitality, originality and openness towards innovation - characteristics of many of these economic contexts in Italy - represents a stimulating opportunity for implementing original innovative solutions by intelligent synergy with the new information technologies. On their part these solutions could turn out to be models transferable to other countries, especially developing ones.

The interest of suppliers of information and telematics equipment (be it hardware or software) in being involved in initiatives of this sort is quite clear. In fact, after the cited examples of Italian communications companies, plans are being worked out for future collaboration with the major multinational information technology organisations, which would provide them with the opportunity for assessing small and medium-sized Italian concerns as an optimal workshop on the world market for the development of specific products and the acquisition of original socio-technical experience.

There are well-known examples of collaboration between information multinationals and major Italian companies, considered world leaders in their sectors, such as by Fiat with Digital and IBM and STET with IBM.

So, a great challenge has been opened up of immense importance and complexity, involving not only technology but, above all, cultural and organisational realities. The challenge has to be accepted and dealt with in a systematic way by all the interested parties - local and national sector associations, local governments, the competent national administrative bodies, the public service bodies, the supplier companies and, finally a body of a proven experience in technical and organisational innovation in the role of catalyst for specific initiatives.

The last-mentioned body, which is clearly the critical element in the situation, should occupy a neutral position with respect to suppliers of hardware and software, be able to carry out the architectural and engineering functions efficiently and in particular, set up as its strategic objective the optimum use of all the possible synergies between different production sectors which may have similarities in product, production process and organisational structure.

ENEA has established itself authoritatively in this field and, as we have already seen, is in a position to offer concrete experience and results to all interested parties.

References

Pyburn, P.J., and Curley, K.F. (1984) 'The evolution of intellectual technologies: applying product life-cycle models to MIS implementation'. *Information and Management*, 7(6).

Media Duemila (1987) 'Quando I' informatica entra in la azienda'. 5(6).

13. Technical information flow in Ireland

Tom Casey

Science Policy Research Centre
University College
Dublin

Information for manufacturing firms

Manufacturing in industrialised countries has been undergoing a number of radical changes since the early 1970s. Two of these changes are of particular interest from the information flow point of view: (1) the relationship of manufacturing with the service industries, usually seen as heavy users of information, is changing; (2) the internal structure and organisation of firms are being transformed by new technology based information flows. This transformation is recognised as a key issue in competitiveness.

Information service subcontracting

Information-rich services such as advertising and legal advice have nearly always been contracted out. They are now being joined by previously internal functions such as recruitment, personnel and strategic management as well as low-information services such as cleaning, catering, clerical and typing work. Manufacturing firms are slimming down to specific core skills where their own competitive advantage is strongest and most defensible, usually in strongly technical areas. They see others as able to marshal, manage and supply services from strategic management to cleaning more efficiently and cheaply than themselves. This reorganisation of the manufacturing sector has been called 'meta-industrialisation' by some French workers (SEMA-METRA 1987). It is essentially a restructuring based on extreme specialisation in certain functions or information areas of the traditional manufacturing firm.

Areas high in technical information content, related to product or process technology, are undergoing a similar change. Product design requires access to, manipulation and management of, and decision-making based on, increasingly large and varied sets of technical information. This pushes the manufacturing firm to incorporate specialist firms into its design work. A striking example is the growth of materials specialist firms. The explosion of available new materials (alloys, composites, ceramics) has increased the set of variables for product design enormously as regards product and manufacturing properties. The mastery and updating of such materials related information would be inefficient for many manufacturing firms. Occasional resort to a specialist firm provides the necessary input.

On the process technology side the growing variety of capital equipment has led to some new service firms. Most important has been the growth of specialised service firms related to the introduction of microelectronic-based process technology. The introduction of microelectronics has posed major new problems and opportunities to firms, large and small alike. Resort to high-quality specialised information is of the utmost importance since we are dealing with areas closely related to what a manufacturing firm considers its 'specific core skills'. Mistakes do not simply result in the purchase of non-optimal units of capital equipment but weaken the essential competitive base of the firm. They also have implications for moves towards integrated manufacture. Mistakes may imply that islands of automation may stay just that or require extremely expensive software bridges.

As well as relying to a greater extent on external technical service firms, Original Equipment Manufacturers, Systems and Component Manufacturers are also increasing subcontracting, using the specialist skills of the subcontractor (a type of technical service firm) to supplement their own competiveness. This also lays off some of the risk of market fluctuations. The subcontractor is also seen as being better able to amortise new equipment through high volume throughput.

This general discussion already poses a problem for less-developed regions' access to the specialised technical information embodied in these new service firms. It is extremely unlikely that such firms will establish within the less-developed regions. Given that geographical distance and cultural difference curtails use of such resources, firms in areas of the EC such as Portugal, Greece and Ireland are at a major disadvantage in using such information. Given the current weak manufacturing base in these areas, the trends outlined above are likely to increase polarisation of manufacturing within the EC.

Impact of information technology

Looking now at information flows within the manufacturing firm, electronic data collection, storage, analysis and communication have opened information treatment generally and technical information in particular to changes which can entail major gains in competitiveness for firms. Electronic data/information treatment within a function such as design has shortened design periods, increased reliability and quality and brought many general advantages of automation. Its operation between functions such as design and manufacture or manufacturing and purchase has again increased reliability and quality, reduced order times and work in progress and so on. It is also becoming important, often essential, as the means of external communications between the manufacturing firm, suppliers and customers. Maximising the opportunities from these developments has not been easy. Success seems to be allied to rethinking the firm's functions and their interrelationships; rethinking the organisation rather than grafting new technologies and systems onto existing functions and structures. Some European Commission workers (EEC 1988) have christened this the 'orgware' of the firm. This parallels a firm's 'hardware' (hard technology) and 'software' (systems and techniques).

Looking at the less developed regions, these developments do not seem as negative as the meta-industrialisation changes. All firms are being challenged to rethink their orgware. It is not evident that firms in developed regions have major skills in breaking out of traditional modes of thought compared to less developed regions.

In summary, the ability of the manufacturing firm to access information, particularly technical information, to analyse it and make appropriate decisions seems to be an increasingly important element of competitiveness. We have also seen some disadvantages to the less-developed regions in accessing specialised technical information embodied in the new technically based service firms.

Industrial structure

Turning to Ireland, the indigenous engineering industries of this country in their firm size, structure and ownership typify the problems of less-developed regions in use of information for competitiveness.

Firm size and sector

Table 13.1 shows the firm size structure of the engineering sector in Europe in terms of employees per establishment. The small firm size structure of Portugal, Greece and Ireland in all sectors should be noted. It is probable that Spain has a similar structure. In the case of Ireland, at least, these figures grossly over estimate the real

Table 13.1 Average number of employees per enterprise in engineering

	Metal Articles Nace 31	Mech. Eng Nace 32	Elect. Eng Nace 34
European Community	94.2	146.6	304
Belgium	83.2	157.8	433
Denmark	76.4	126.7	180
West Germany	126.0	210.2	408
France	91.8	128.0	293
Ireland	59.0	79.0	137
Italy	62.7	96.2	193
Luxemburg	65.0	195.0	103
Netherlands	70.2	90.0	459
United Kingdom	103.7	142.5	294
Greece	80.9	39.1	44
Spain	compatible figures not available		
Portugal	53.7	61.7	162

average size of firms. Official statistics show the average firm size to be somewhere in the region of twenty to thirty people. In terms of indigenous Irish industry this is again an overestimate since most large firm industry in Ireland is foreign owned.

Table 13.2 shows two other important features of industrial structure in the small, peripheral countries of Europe; the small overall size of the engineering industry and its concentration in the lower skilled and lower value added sectors. Ireland, Greece,

Table 13.2 Share of industries in total number of persons employed in manufacturing

	Metal Articles Nace 31	Mech. Eng Nace 32	Office/Data Nace 33	Elect. Eng Nace 34
European Community	9.0	10.9	1.0	12.3
Belgium	6.5	8.3	0.2	10.5
Denmark	7.2	15.0	0.3	9.2
West Germany	9.2	14.3	1.1	14.0
France	10.7	6.5	1.2	11.9
Ireland	5.5	3.3	3.3	8.5
Italy	8.5	10.6	1.2	11.5
Luxemburg	5.3	9.2	-	4.0
Netherlands	8.1	9.6	-	14.4
United Kingdom	8.0	10.8	0.8	11.4
Greece	5.6	2.1	-	5.1
Spain	11.5	5.2	0.1	6.0
Portugal	7.2	3.1	0.3	5.0

Portugal and to a lesser extent Spain have lower proportions of total employment in the main engineering sectors than the other countries. (The high level of Irish employment in Office and Data Processing Machinery is due to massive US Multinational investment). Also notable is the concentration of the same countries' engineering in the low skilled Metal Articles sector and the weakness in the more traded and more skilled Mechanical and Electrical Engineering sectors.

These basic features of industrial structure; low proportion of employment in engineering (and manufacturing in general), small-size structure of firms and concentration in the low-skill sectors have important consequences for technical information flow from external sources. Looking first at firm size structure, Table 13.3 shows the percentage of indigenous engineering firms in a survey who received any technical assistance or advice from external sources according to firm size. As can be seen there is a consistent increase in the use of external sources as the size of firm increases. Small firms find it more difficult to access external technical assistance/advice and external sources wishing to impart technical assistance/advice find it more difficult to access such firms.

Table 13.3 Use of any assistance or advice by firm size

Size	1-15	16-50	51-100	101-200	+201	Total
Yes	56%	79%	88%	91%	100%	71%
No	44%	21%	12%	9%	0%	29%

(number of firms = 259)

Second, the concentration of industry in the lower-value-added/less-skilled sectors implies that the type technical assistance/advice the firms require or at least are able to accept and implement is fairly basic in nature. Third, given the size structure of industry, it is doubtful if more than 5 per cent of indigenous firms could afford to use any of the new specialist technical information firms discussed earlier. Fourth, and perhaps most importantly, the size structure of industry poses a question as to the ability of these firms to exploit commercially any technical information which they receive.

Occupation structure

The occupational structure of firms is reflected to some extent in the number of qualified scientists and engineers per 10,000 population in various countries shown in Table 13.4. The figure in brackets for Ireland shows the number of scientists engineers *and* technicans per 10,000 population. Table 4 overestimates the relative strength of qualified technical manpower in Irish industry since a greater proportion of such manpower work in government establishments in less developed countries than in developed countries.

Table 13.4. Qualified scientists and engineers per 10,000 population

Ireland	88	(104)
Denmark	163	
Austria	205	
France	237	
Norway	238	
Sweden	404	

Source: UNESCO figures for 1981

A second indicator of the technical manpower in firms in less-developed regions is the ratio of business R & D to gross value added. This is shown in Table 13.5. These two indications point to the relative weakness of qualified technical manpower in industry in less developed regions. In the case of the Irish engineering industry the proportion of engineers is about 1.5 per cent, while the figure for the technicians approaches 3 per cent of industry employment. Overall, only about one in six firms have engineers, while one in four have technicians. These figures are slightly lower for indigenous firms.

Table 13.5. Ratio of business R & D to gross value added

West Germany	2.19
Belgium	1.5
Denmark	1.0
Portugal	0.6
Ireland	0.4

Source: NBST (1987)

The low proportion of qualified technical manpower in Irish indigenous industry presents another major fundamental obstacle to the flow of technical information into these firms. There must be a recognition of the importance of technical information and an ability to understand and incorporate such information into the firm before technical information is of any potential use to the firm. These recognition and incorporation processes are severely handicapped by the absence of qualified technical manpower from the firms of the less-developed regions of Europe. EC programmes which promote higher levels of technically qualified people in firms in the less-developed regions make an important contribution to improving technical information flow into these regions.

Ownership structure

Within Ireland, a high level of manufacturing employment is provided by the subsidiaries of multinational firms. This varies from 80-90 per cent in sectors of fine chemicals, pharmaceuticals and electronics to 50 per cent in the traditional engineering sector to lower levels in traditional sectors such as textiles, food processing and so on. The presence of these subsidiaries present a potential for technical information flows to indigenous industry either though new firm start-ups, staff mobility or subcontracting work.

A major effort has been made over the last three years to increase the level of indigenous firms subcontracting to foreign firms through the National Linkage Programme. While technical information flow is evident through individual cases of vendor engineering, the overall impact of the programme in this area is still unclear.

Some work has been done on supervisory and managerial staff mobility from foreign electronic firms to indigenous industry (Onyenadum and Tomlin 1984). This study indicated that 'The companies selected for the study showed significant potential as sources of technology'. The study followed the career patterns of eighty-two people who had left two large foreign multinationals over a ten year period. In their current organisations 60 per cent were still with foreign companies, 10 per cent had started a company, while 18 per cent were with state or educational organisations, leaving 12 per cent in indigenous companies., The latter is not an encouraging result. New firm formation at 10 per cent of former employees, however, is extremely high. Of the eight companies, three were in services and five in manufacturing. While none were in 'high-tech' sectors, they must be regarded as important in the sense of technical information transfer.

Another study of firms in the indigenous electronics industry found about 17 per cent (six out of thirty-five) were spin-off firms from foreign electronics firms (Cogan and Onyenadum 1981).

In all, the presence of multinational subsidiaries presents a positive force for technology information flows. New firm start-ups rather than staff mobility to indigenous firms seems to be the major avenue for technical information flow. To some extent this is explained by the very low level of qualified technical manpower in existing indigenous industry, the low proportion of the total industry which is in indigenous hands and its low attraction for skilled engineers. It is possible that technical information flows from foreign to indigenous industry via staff mobility is higher in traditional industries. There are, however, no Irish studies to support or disprove this.

Summarising, the firm and occupational structure of indigenous manufacturing in less-developed regions present major problems to transferring technical information of commercial worth. New ways of dealing with such structures must be designed. Unfortunately, what these 'new ways' are is not that obvious. The ownership structure of Irish industry, from the point of view of technical information flow at least, seems positive. Information flow to indigenous industry seems greater from start-ups than staff mobility.

Technical advice/support to the individual firm

In examining the flow of technical advice/support to individual engineering firms, comparison of the differences in flows between indigenous and the supposedly more cosmopolitan foreign subsidiaries in Ireland shows some sharp contrasts

Table 13.6 indicates that foreign firms showed a greater propensity to use *all* external resources. This is explained mainly by the firm size structure of the sample. The ratio of foreign to indigenous firm use of a resource is given in the third column. Most notable is the major support from parent and sister companies available to foreign firms. A second point to note is the greater use

Table 13.6. Percentages of indigenous and foreign firms using different sources of technical advice/assistance

	Indigenous Firms	Foreign Firms	Ratio	Usefulness
Equipment suppliers	42	53	1.3	63
Equipment manufacturers	30	56	1.9	68
Parent/sister company	4	75	18.8	80
Other company	7	9	1.3	61
University	6	15	2.5	38
Regional technical colleges	6	11	2.5	24
National Institute of Higher Education	4	14	3.5	36
College of Technology	3	7	2.3	63
Consultants	10	12	1.2	58
EOLAS (Science and Technology Agency	46	48	1.0	49
FAS (Training and Employment Authority)	32	42	1.3	47

Number of indigenous firms = 259 Number of foreign firms = 120 made of higher education resources by foreign firms. Indigenous firms have a relatively greater reliance on state sources (EOLAS and FAS) of advice and assistance. A final point to note is the greater reliance of indigenous firms on equipment suppliers than the actual manufacturers.

Firms were also asked how useful they found the technical advice/support they received from the particular source. Firms could reply 'essential' 'useful' or 'not useful'. In fact no firm judged any source 'not useful'. An indicator of usefulness was constructed by simply taking the percentage of 'essential' responses to total responses. These percentages are shown in the fourth column. They show technical advice/support from parent or sister companies to be most useful. At a second order of 'usefulness' comes other firms: suppliers, manufacturers, consultants and other firms generally. The third group includes state agencies while the fourth group includes higher education-institutes. Other sources such as customers, trade fairs and trade magazines are not captured in this data. With this general background of the relative importance of technical advice/support sources we now briefly examine some of the issues particular to each source in the context of Ireland as a less developed region of Europe.

Higher education

The direct importance of higher education to industrial development may have been over-estimated to some extent over the 1980s. While it does produce new high-tech start-ups, science parks, teaching companies, consultancy and so on, its overall direct impact on industrial structure and employment is not great. Its major impact will continue to be, as it always has been, the quality of the people it trains. Table 13.4 backs this assertion to some extent.

A number of documents have examined the higher education/industry interface in Ireland over the 1980s. Many of their conclusions would be similar to those in developed regions of Europe: too academic, insufficient staff mobility, legislation and practices which restrict consultancy and so on. In the less-developed regions of Europe additional problems, however, arise which handicap the flow of technical information/support from higher education and to indigenous industry.

The orientation of higher education, particularly university education, towards high/breakthrough/frontier technologies rather than applications/development technologies represents a greater handicap to less-developed compared to developed regions. In the former the firms which can develop and exploit such technologies simply do not exist.

A similar criticism can be made of the EEC's precompetitive research programmes where the small indigenous firms of less developed regions are usually in no position to commercialise the resultant research work. Indeed, Table 13.4 shows that the universities and NIHE's link in more firmly to foreign subsidiaries where there is a 'higher' technology. The regional technical colleges, essentially 'lower' technology and more applications orientated, give relatively better value to indigenous industry.

The spread and depth of technical information/support that can be drawn on in higher education also presents relatively greater problems in countries such as Ireland, Greece and Portugal.

State agencies

Generally, state agencies represent a proportionally greater store of technical information in less-developed regions than in the developed regions, where private and public firms are larger, more technically sophisticated and perform a greater proportion of R & D. It would also appear from Table 13.4, that they give a more even treatment to indigenous and foreign firms compared to higher education.

As with higher education, many problems of state agencies are similar to those in developed regions; low staff mobility, ageing staff structures, inadequate capital equipment, and so on. Particular problems in less-developed regions seem to be related to maintaining the scope of expertise.

Other companies

Other companies, particularly manufacturers and suppliers of equipment, are the major source of technical support/advice to manufacturing firms and are also thought to be the most useful source. As such they are a crucial part of the industrial infrastructure through which technical information passes. They present themselves as a possible point to gain leverage in improving the quality of manufacturing generally in less-developed regions.

It is currently being suggested to Directorate General V, Social Policy, of the Commission of the European Communities, working on the human resources aspects of technical change, that greater attention be given to training/updating of equipment suppliers, distributors, agents (and indeed the possibility of training using these groups) as such a key element in the manufacturing 'ecology' of a region. The possibilities of piggy-backing improved technical information flows along such lines might be considered also by EC and national governments of less-developed regions.

Technical information and peripheral location

Technical information flow is not simply technical data or blue prints as this chapter has unflinchingly assumed up to now. The craft and tacit nature of much scientific and technical information has been pointed out by many authors. Richard Nelson in particular has talked of the 'codafiability' of a technology as the level to which it can non-ambiguously be written down and transmitted (Nelson 1980) Nathan Rosenberg points to the major importance in technological development of learning by doing (Rosenberg 1982). Manufacturing firms by their very operation generate technical information which may prove extremely difficult to transfer in any formal way to other firms.

Hitchens and O'Farrell (1988) have done important work in this context, comparing manufacturing in different regions of the British Isles. They showed the products of small indigenous companies to matched companies in other regions and asked for their comments on the pricing and quality of the products. The products of the mid-west and North of Ireland were generally felt to be of a poor quality by firms from the mainland UK, particularly firms in south-east England. Firms in Ireland, on the other hand, tended to find all products satisfactory. When they did find fault they were less definite in describing the fault. In Ireland firms run by foreigners or ex-employees of multinational firms suffered less criticism than fully indigenous firms. Interestingly, capital equipment in Irish firms was generally newer than that of counterparts on the UK mainland. This work points to the fundamental difficulty of transmitting such basic technical information as quality requirements into manufacturing firms distant from the main manufacturing centres and outside the main flows of tacit/ contact information.

Similar, less empirical, opinions are expressed on the craft nature of both high- and low-level technical information and its weakness in Ireland by foreign nationals working in Ireland (Petersen 1987). Such work points not only to the difficulty of transmission of technical information to the peripheral areas but also the need for a far more sophisticated approach than simply the installation of high-power information transmission systems. Equally, if not more important than the transmission of 'hard' technical information is the transmission of craft/tacit technical knowledge.

Some EEC programmes such as COMETT consciously or unconsciously recognise this situation, providing for the exchange of personnel between firms for extended periods of time. In terms of technical information flow such elements of programmes deserve a much greater proportion of expenditure. Much current EC thinking, however, seems to believe that building powerful broadband ISDN communications highways into less developed regions answers many of the technical information flow issues and gives a base development.

From what we have said in this chapter, the former is highly questionable. As for acting as a base for development, one might ask, 'Whose development: the firms of the less-developed regions or the major firms who will supply the hard technology?' If it is indeed firms of the less-developed regions, it is questionable, given the discussions above, whether they have the resources to use this highway. It is also questionable whether they have anything to put on this highway. Indeed, one might even be unsure as to which way the value added will flow along these highways. Might value added actually flow out of less-developed regions along these highways - a new form of emigration?

Joint ventures, licensing and the transfer of technical information

This section is based on some fifty case studies carried out over the period 1982-7 by students of Master's of Industrial Engineering, University College, Dublin under the direction of Mel Healy and the present author.

Joint ventures and licensing/know-how agreements are an extremely powerful method for the transfer of technical information to developing regions. The case of Japan during the 1950s and 1960s is often quoted. Recognition of this potential by European governments and the EC has been relatively slow. Our case studies point to a number of issues which may be of interest as regards use and importance in the context of joint ventures and licensing agreements. We do not have pretensions to any academic rigour, however.

1. Initial product information and technical information is nearly always sought in highly specialised industry sectors, where the entrepreneur or small firm has particular experience. Nearly all case studies show joint ventures or licensing being undertaken within the very specific area in which the entrepreneur or small company is working. This is partly for credibility with the licensor, partly to build existing marketing and production skills. For government agencies to supply such industry specific, even product specific information to firms seems near impossible. They can only act in a motivating and support role.
2. Market information is usually required before technical information. A common source of licensing and joint venture agreements is the move from being an agent or distributor to manufacturing one or more of the products in Ireland. The market for the product is established so that the risks of moving into manufacture are then

substantially lower. There is, also, a major difference in corporation tax on manufacturing (10 per cent) compared to distribution (50 per cent) profits in Ireland. Another indication of the early importance of market information is that potential licensors often require the licensee to distribute the product for a set period, meeting certain volume and service requirements before completing licensing. This again points to agents and distributors as a strong information/industrial development force in less-developed regions.

3. The major transfers of technical information (the setting up and initial manufacturing runs) give occasional problems but are not an area for concern. It is striking that only one of the case studies comments on this as a major problem. The array of technical information transfer mechanisms integrated and focused on a specific area make licensing one of the surest ways to transfer both tacit and explicit information. Training of licensees' engineers by licensor, loan of key personnel to licensee at start-up, assistance with purchase and maintenance of machinery, initial supply of awkward parts or components by licensor and so on, guarantee the transfer of the technology.
4. Failure in licensing or joint ventures does not seem strongly related to insufficient technical information. Only a few case studies have related failure or potential failure. These focus mostly on the initial search being a failure. One large dairy co-operative sought a license for dairy products in the US not realising that the European dairy products market is a number of years ahead of the USA. Another firm after sourcing a potential product found, on analysis of competition, that it would not be able to gain sufficient market share. Failure during the life time of the agreement seems to relate to commercial issues rather than technical issues. Change of management in the licensor causes difficulties, fall in the value of the dollar undermines the raison d'être of the joint venture and so on. These failures underline the fact that technology and technical information are not things-in-themselves but are only important within a commercial framework. The provision of technical information to firms is pointless unless it is focused through commercial plans.
5. Government action can improve the use of technical and market information by small firms, particularly in the initial stages of licensing and joint ventures. This point is worth considering in some detail. The case studies which form the base for this chapter cover the beginning of an important shift in Irish industrial policy from emphasis on the settlement of multinational subsidiaries in Ireland to the development of indigenous industry. In particular, 1985-6 saw the launch of the Industrial Development Authority's Technology Transfer Programme. The effects of this programme can be detected in the case studies.

Regarding the final issue here, initial case studies, before IDA intervention, show a marked contrast between large and small firms in dealing with technical information. Small firms (under seventy-five employees) were much more likely to move into licensing or joint ventures based on the acquisition of 'chance' information: information from meetings at trade fairs, information from customers or suppliers etc. Initial idea/assessment of the project was done quickly and informally. This contrasted with large firms (mostly the dairy co-operatives) who, having adequate resources, were even then undertaking formalised searches and assessment of products.

Since the initiation of the IDA's Technology Transfer Programme and the associated Technology Acquisition Grants, small firms have been required while seeking grants to obtain and structure a great level of technical and market information and to formalise search and assessment procedures. This has permitted the firms to make informed and explicit judgements on issues such as patent strength, market share, competitors etc.

The period 1984-7 has also seen changes in the administration of the Programme which may be of interest. The high early failure rate (companies in difficulty were using the Programme as a 'last straw') reorientated the IDA away from working with weak companies. The success rate rose quite dramatically. Great emphasis was placed on the quality of the projects causing the annual average sales per project to nearly double in the 1984-6 period. The programme was also devolved from a centralised unit to operational divisions so that it is more fully integrated into company development. In all the IDA programme has increased the level and quality of licensing and joint ventures and, through this, improved technical information flow into Ireland.

Conclusions

Rather than bringing together all the small conclusions and policy implications of this paper, I would like to repeat what I feel are the three key points regarding technical information flow to manufacturing firms in the less developed regions.

1. The major issue in technical information flow or support into less-developed regions is how to cope with industry structures of very small firms and low skills. Very small firms cannot be ignored. In less developed regions they make up 75 per cent of indigenous employment in most sectors. If they collapse under increased competition with completion of the internal market, it will negate any moves towards EC cohesion. Unemployment in the less developed regions will further polarise the EC.
2. Technical information has a large tacit element which is often neglected in providing technical support to firms outside the main flow of the technical culture of the developed regions.
3. Equipment suppliers, distributors and agents are a resource that might be exploited to a much greater extent. They combine market

and technical knowledge along with credible contacts with manufacturers in the less developed regions and sophisticated manufacturers outside the region.

References

Cogan, D. J. and Onyenadum, E. (1981) 'Spin-off companies in the Irish electronics industry'. *Journal of Irish Business and Administration Research* 3(2).

EEC (1988) *Human Work Technology and Industrial Strategies: Options for Europe*. Brussels: FAST Programme.

Hitchens, D. M. W. N., and O'Farrell, P. (1988) *The Comparative Performance of Small Manufacturing Companies in Ireland: A Matched Comparison of Firms Located in N. Ireland and the Mid West*. University of Belfast: mimeo.

NBST (1987). *Science and Technology for Regional Innovation and Development in Europe*. Brussels: EEC.

Nelson, R.R. (1980) 'Production sets, technological knowledge and R & D: fragile and overworked constructs for analysis of productivity growth?' *American Economic Review*, 70 (2).

Onyenadum, E., and Tomlin, B. (1984) 'Technology transfer through staff mobility.' *Journal of Irish Business and Administrative Research* 6 (1 and 2).

Petersen, F. P. (1987) 'Running a business in Ireland', Meeting on Danish marketing strategy. Dublin, Industrial Studies Association.

Rosenberg, N. (1982) *'Inside the Black Box: Technology and Economics.'* Cambridge: Cambridge University Press.

Sema Metra (1987) *Services to the Manufacuring Sector: A Long Term Investigation*. Brussels: FAST FOP no. 96.

Sweeney, G. P. (1985) *Study on Information Networks Designed to Support Technological Innovation in Less-Favoured Regions of the Community*. Dublin: IIRS. 5 volumes.

14. The location of information intensive economic activities in the European Community

W. Molle, L. Beumer and I. Boeckhout

Netherlands Economic Institute
Rotterdam

Information and regional development: the problem

The European Community is confronted with considerable problems of regional imbalance (CEC 1987). The problems are generally measured by the disparities which exist among regions in terms of welfare, in practice gross domestic product per head. We have shown elsewhere (Molle *et al.* 1980; Molle and van Haselen 1987), that these disparities have gradually decreased since the Second World War, as a result of:

1. the gradual dispersion of industrial activity;
2. migration of people from the poorer to the richer regions; and also
3. a better distribution of commercial and welfare-state services (Molle and Van Holst, 1984; Molle, 1986).

Moreover regional policy is supposed to have contributed to an improved regional balance. However, the impact of other EC policies on the regional equilibrium (agricultural policy, for instance), has sometimes been negative (Molle and Cappellin, 1988).

Recently, considerable attention has been focused on the impact of technology on the economy in general and the relation between technology and regional development in particular. A first analysis of that relation was the PRESTO study carried out for the European Community in the framework of the FAST-I programme (Molle 1983). This study singled out information and telecommunication as key areas for action.

Indeed, modern means of telecommunication (electronic mail, videotex, tele-conferencing, data transmission) have made information activities (generally carried on in offices) potentially more footloose and earier to split up than before. The assumption of the PRESTO study was that the successful exploitation of that potential depends presumably on the communication infrastructure, which at the time was far from equally developed in all European regions.

The present chapter sets out to throw some light on the development potential of regions by studying the location preferences of two highly information-intensive activities: head offices, and research and development. The location of corporate headquarters (HQ) is the first element to study. The increased integration on the European and world levels has stimulated the formation of giant multinational companies controlling a large number of affiliate companies. The entailing spatial differentiation is evident from the regional economies' increasing dependence on outside control (see, among others, Smith 1979; Lloyd and Dicken 1977; Firn 1975; Keizer 1974). The location of the control functions, usually carried on in the HQ of the multinationals, is particularly relevant, information being a key factor of location. We will see that the tendency to concentrate these activities in large urban centres is still strong.

The location of R & D activities is the next point to explore. The specific role of information with respect to these activities requires a different set of location factors. We will see, however, that R & D, like HQ, clearly prefer spatial concentration. By a variant of multicriteria analysis we will try to establish how the top ten locations for HQ and R&D have come by their relative positions.

Head offices and related functions

Some theory

Most of the work on office location has been done on the intra-urban level (e.g. by Beumer *et al.* 1984), while we are interested particularly in the inter-urban location pattern. Most of the few empirical studies available for Europe (Ahnstrom 1973; Dunning and Norman 1979; IIM 1981) are based on the theory of the multinational firm (e.g. Lloyd and Dicken 1977). Recently a number of contributions to the theory of head office location have been made (by ter Hart 1980; Dunning and Norman 1983; Coffey and Polese 1983; and others), from which emerges a certain consensus about the factors determining the choice of locations of head offices. We have picked out the Coffey/Polese approach, which is based on the following assumptions (validated via various techniques):

1. Every head office procedures a set of varied and variable outputs; there is a captive market (CM) for each output in the form of the plants of affiliate companies. The demand is geographically distributed according to the multi-regional and multinational pattern of branch establishements and affiliate companies.
2. To function well, HQ need two inputs: Advances Corporate Services (ACS) and Skilled Management Resources (SMR). With two inputs

and one output variable the location of HQ can graphically be represented in a triangle (Fig. 14.1).

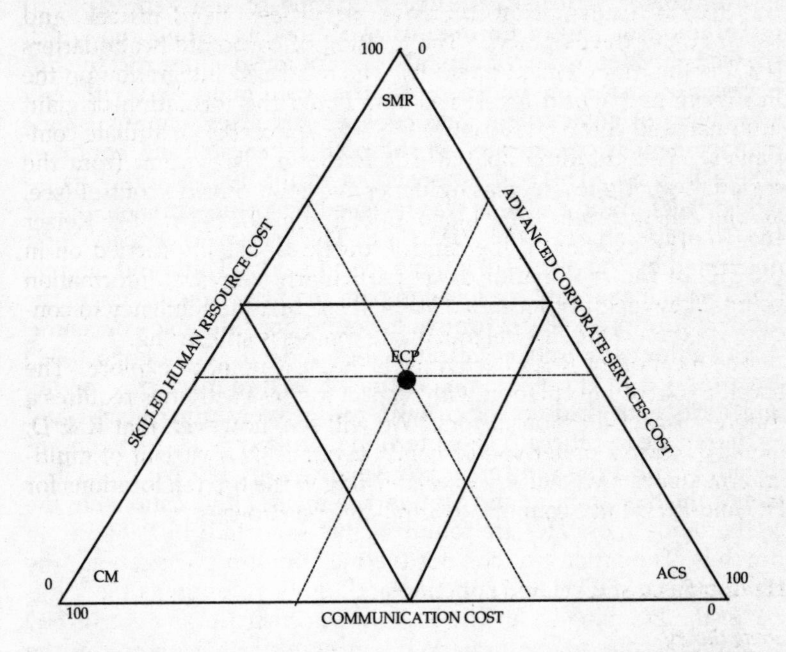

Figure 14.1 A typology of head office location *source:* Coffey and Polese 1983

If a HQ spends more on one of these facilities than on the other two, its location may be assumed to be fully determined by that factor (one of three extreme triangles). If not, there is a flexible choice of locations (central triangle around the point of equal cost proportions (ECP)).

The three dominant types for Europe can be illustrated as follows:

1. SMR locations are cities that either have specialised labour pools or offer a high quality of life; cities like Nice, Lyon-Grenoble, Munich come to mind.
2. ACS locations imply a greater externalisation of inputs requiring large corporate office complexes. In Europe, cities like London, Paris and Frankfurt qualify.
3. CM locations imply a good situation in a network of telecom and passenger transport services. In many cases these cities are the same as the ones under item 2, with some smaller ones like Amsterdam thrown in.

European manufacturing firms

A number of studies produce evidence of the geographical distribution of HQ in Europe. An early one by Ahnstrom (1973) showed the hierarchies of capital and provincial cities, and the differences on that score between countries with many and with only few layers of government, and between countries where business management is oncentrated in the political capital and coutnries where it is not. The pattern observed in the 1960s largely maintained itslef in the 1970s, as was revealed by a study carried out for the Commission of the EC (IIM 1981). This pattern is probably best illustrated by the results of a more recent study (Thuis and de Jong 1983), which analysed the location pattern of the head offices of the top 500 European (EC9) firms and found considerable concentration in a limited number of capital cities. Indeed, 306 out of 500 HQ were located in cities accommodating at least four others. London and Paris take pride of place with respectively ninety-eight and sixty-four head offices. The pattern in Germany is far less concentrated; besides the centres of Nordrhein-Westfalen we find cities like Munich, Hamburg and Stuttgart as major HQ locations. In the Netherlands most HQ are found in the Randstad; in Belgium, in Brussels. The latter city has not (yet) acquired a place among the top European HQ cities, notwithstanding its vocation as the 'capital' of the EC. Finally, no city in Italy has emerged as a major HQ location in spite of the remarkable growth of its economy in the post-war era.

The picture becomes sharper if one looks not only at the number of HQ but also at the total employment. London then appears by far the most important European city (with a total of 4.5 million), followed at a distance by Paris (2.3 million) and Dusseldorf (1 million). All other centres control fewer than 0.5 million employees. This concentration on London appears to be very much on the ACS specialist services and SMR skilled labour factors, (Dunning and Norman 1979).

As far as the Advanced Corporate Services are concerned, the primacy of London is clear. Indeed, the city of London is one of the world's few leading centres for financial intermediation, and the world's largest insurance centre, attracting many related financial services to it (McRae and Cairncross 1984). Another illustration of the function of London is the location of the large accountancy firms; six of the 'big nine' world-wide firms have their major roots as well as their major European offices in the city of London (Leyshon *et al.*1987).

In London and the other major European cities, there is a close association between ACS and SMR functions. An analysis of the concentration of highly-qualified non-manual workers in service industries in the EC (Cameron *et al.* 1981) reveals a pattern similar to that of ACS. SMR indeed show considerable concentration is the south-east of the UK and in the Paris region, while in the other countries they are far less concentrated. De Jong and Thuis 1983 have also analysed the location of the plants controlled by each HQ, in terms of the influence of the cost of communication with the captive market (CM). They found that the CM factor was very important indeed; as a matter of fact almost half of the total number of employees controlled by a HQ work in plants at less than 100 km from the HQ. The figure varies somewhat from sector to sector; steel and metal are highly concentrated, automobiles and chemicals show average distances from HQ to plants, while electronics show a wide dispersion (long distances between HQ and plants).

Finally, we want to stress the close association of the head office function with a number of other international information intensive activities like communications, trade fairs and international congresses, recently established in a study performed by a group of geographers from Montpellier (RECLUS 1987). Their study, which focused on cities with over 200,000 inhabitants, showed again the concentration of these activities in a belt running from the Midlands of England to Rome, with a number of cities in countries like Spain and Denmark providing a certain counterweight.

Non-European firms

The European market has become very important to non-European firms. Some of these firms have decided to establish not only sales companies but also production facilities in Europe. Their activities have reached such a volume that they can no longer be efficiently managed by corporate headquarters (CHQ) in the USA or Japan, and regional (European) headquarters (RHQ) are judged necessary. The locational needs of these RHQ reflect their role as co-ordinators of the activities of the firms' European affiliates and transmitters of instructions from CHQ to the affiliates. Hence they represent a specific combination of the general factors mentioned in the previous section. The key factor of location is often is often easy access to a set of contact points, which in practice means a location close to an international airport providing a multitude of links with frequent flights.

The location patterns of the US and Japanese RHQ are quite different:

1. The pattern of US RHQ is fairly similar to the one for European firms, but Brussels is far more important to the former than to the latter. The central location of that city combined with the presence of

the EC administration with its emerging complex of specialist legal services may have been decisive.

2. Japanese RHQ are highly concentrated. Also for then London is a key location, but the main concentration point is Dusseldorf. The preference is essentially of a social-cultural nature. The initial location of Japanese firms in the most important city of the dominant area in the country that has become the strongest economic power of Europe, has laid the foundation for Japanese education and social facilities, which attract new firms to it.

A ranking of cities and locations for HQ

We have analysed in some more detail the various location factors of HQ, specifying some of the elements that had been discussed in general terms in the studies cited before. To the CM, ACS and SMR functions we added three other criteria: the legal and fiscal situation, the quality of the environment, and the quality of the accommodation. Next we established the scores by the six criteria of the following cities: London, Paris, Hamburg, Brussels, Frankfurt, Munchen and Randstad Holland, ranking the cities by the results. A score one means very good, a seven implies that the location ranks last by the criterion in question. The information thus obtained was then subjected to the Qualiflex multicritéria method; Table 14.1 presents the detailed results. The final general ranking is as follows (Boeckhout *et al.* 1987):

1 London
2 Paris
3/4 Brussels, Randstad
5/6 Frankfurt, Munich
7 Hamburg

This ranking is very stable; changes in the sets of weights hardly affect the values and do not change the ranking.

The emerging picture confirms the findings of previous studies. London and Paris owe their positions largely to the factors already mentioned: high-quality services (ASC), good quality of the environment and hence of staff (SMR) and communication (CM). London profits in particular from the cheap fees for bulk telecommunication and the low corporate taxes prevailing there.

Research and development

The nature of the activity

R & D is the first step towards innovation of a product and/or production process. Innovation is a key element to any firm, whether it takes the form of advanced fundamental research relying on basic

Table 14.1 Location factors of head offices: scores of cities

Rank	Location factor	Rand-stad	London	Paris	Hamburg	Frank-furt	Munich	Brussels/ Antwerp
	Infrastructure and accessibility (CM)							
1	- international airport	x						
2	- quality and efficiency of the services on the airport	1	4	3	6	2	7	5
3	- attainable for cars	x						
3	- sufficient parking	x						
	- communication facilities	x						
3	- quality of telecommunication	7	1	2	3-6	3-6	3-6	3-6
3	- tariffs of telecommunication	3	1	4	5/6/7	5/6/7	5/6/7	2
	Agglomeration (ACS)							
1	- other head offices	4	2	1	5/6	7	5/6	3
1	- high-level professional services	5	1	2	7	3	6	4
2	- political, business centre	4	2/3	2/3	5/6/7	5/6/7	5/6/7	1
	Labour market (SMR)							
2	highly qualified manpower	4	7	6	1/2/3	1/2/3	1/2/3	5
	Quality of accommodation							
2	- social and cultural services	3/4	1/2	1/2	5/6/7	5/6/7	5/6/7	3/4
2	- high-level educational services	3	1	2	5/6/7	5/6/7	5/6/7	4
2	- hotel accommodation	x						
2	- residential quality	5	1/2	1/2	6/7	6/7	3/4	3/4
	Legal environment							
1	- fiscal legislation	2	1	7	4/5/6	4/5/6	4/5/6	3
1	- other	5	1	7	2/3/4	2/3/4	2/3/4	6
4	- acquisition	2	1	7	4-7	4-7	3	
3	- political stability	4	6	5	1/2/3	1/2/3	1/2/3	7
	Quality of environment							
4	- premises							
4	- representative offices	5	1/2	1/2	6/7	6/7	4	3
5	- lunch facilities	x						
5	- price level of territory	7	1	5/6	2/3/4	2/3/4	5/6	
5	- prices of offices	2	3	7	4/5/6	4/5/6	4/5/6	1

x An empty row means that all regions have been given the average score of 4; the criterion concerned has no distinctive quality.

innovations, or of the adoption of outside technology to meet new product specifications. There is a strong association between the level of 'in-house' R & D and the speed of adoption of new processes, on the plant as well as the corporate level: firms that are weak in R & D will be weak in innovation and hence have poor long-term growth potentials. R & D activities encompass a variety of tasks. Dependent on their stage in the process they have different locational requirements. (We distinguish three broad stages: Boeckhout *et al.* 1987).

1. *Basic scientific and strategic research (BSSR)* Access to sources of information (universities, other R & D institutes, associations, data banks, etc.) is very important. BSSR activities are often carried on in centres that are also close to corporate headquarters for strategic decision-making and to the R & D infrastructure for fast and easy face-to-face contracts and a good environment to attract high-quality research staff.
2. *Design and development (D & D)* At this stage a good supply of highly qualified staff (researchers and engineers) is a strategic factor. D & D are usually carried on in some relation to the production plant for which the product is destined.
3. *Improvement and adaptation (IA)* This last stage is completely oriented to the marketing needs of the product. Hence the first concern is to have fast access to specialists able to project the demands of the principal customers. This does not mean integration of R & D in the production plant; in fact, some distance is often thought preferable.

From a number of empirical studies we have extracted a list of location requirements of R & D establishments; it is reproduced in Table 14.2.

Concentration tendencies?

Recently the European Commission has launched the STRIDE programme, which is an acronym for Science and Technology for Regional Innovation and Development in Europe. This programme is based on reports of national experts on the R & D performance of all EC regions. Regional BERD and GERD figures were collected for the first time (NBST). GERD (Gross Expenditure on R & D) reflects the total level of R & D being performed by all sectors in the region, higher education institutions, government and private non-profit laboratories, and business enterprise; BERD (Business Expenditure on R & D) reflects the level of R & D in business enterprise only.

Some 80 per cent of European GERD was found to be concentrated in Germany, France and the UK, which shows a considerable spatial concentration for the EC as a whole. The distribution is as uneven in the EC member states Spain, Italy and Denmark. The southern part of France has become a counterweight against the concentration in the Paris region. In the UK (Howells 1984), there is concentration in the residentially attractive areas surrounding the main centres (particularly London): indeed, some 60 per cent of R & D employment of the UK is in the south east).

Multinational corporations (MNC) are paramount in the totality of R & D activities; their influence on the location patterns of R & D is therefore great. Most R & D activities of these MNC are carried on in the home country. Empirical studies (Malecki 1984) indicate that R & D establishments are capital-intensive, which leads to a low mobility of capital and hence quite stable locations, leaving but limited potential for regional development. On the other hand we observe that may firms tend to maintain basic research at 'central' locations while deconcentrating the development activities to the plant level.

A ranking of locations

In the same way as for HQ, we have made a detailed list of the location factors of R & D activities, and established the scores of the seven selected urban centres in Europe on each factor. Again a score 1 means very good, a 7 implies that the location ranks last in the range. Table 14.2 resumes the information gathered. In some cases the information used is national rather than regional, regional data on the factors concerned being very scarce.

Again we have applied the Qualiflex method to these data, which produced the followig ranking for R & D activities.

1 London
2/5 Paris, Frankfurt, Munich, Hamburg
6/7 Randstad, Brussels

Again the ranking reflects largely the situation found in the NBST study. One remarkable difference, however, is that the German cities, ranking first as a group in the NBST study, emerge in second place from our analysis.

We expect the internationalising tendencies to continue, and foresee, therefore, that R & D establishments will become increasingly footloose. If that expectation comes true, the UK with its good general fiscal and regulatory climate and its still low telecommunication tariffs will be in a good position to attract new R & D facilities.

Table 14.2 Location factors R & D activities: scores: of cities

Rank	Location factor	Rand-stad	London	Paris	Hamburg	Frank-furt	Munich	Brussels/ Antwerp
	Infrastructure and accessibility (CM)							
1	- universities & research institutes	x						
4	- international airport	x						
5	- attainable by car	x						
5	- sufficient parking	x						
4	- communication facilities	x]						
5	- quality of telecommunication	7	1	2	3-6	3-6	3-6	3-6
5	- tariffs of telecommunication	3	1	4	5/6/7	5/6/7	5/6/7	2
1	- volume R & D sector	6	4	5	1/2/3	1/2/3	1/2/3	7
	Factor of internal business							
3	- (European) head offices	x agglomeration factor						
3	- product location		'	'				
3	- volume of market	6	5	4	1/2/3	1/2/3	1/2/3	7
3	- European market	3/4	7	2	5/6	1	5/6	3/4
4	- marketing or sales department	x agglomeration factor						
	Labour market (SMR)							
2	highly qualified manpower	6	5	4	1/2/3	1/2/3	1/2/3	7
	Fiscal environment							
4	- fiscal legislation	2	1	7	4/5/6/	4/5/6	4/5/6	3
2	- investment legislation	7	2/3	1	4/5/6	4/5/6	4/5/6	2/3
2	- available venture capital	2	1	7	4/5/6	4/5/6	4/5/6	3
	Quality of environment							
3	- social/cultural services	3/4	1/2	1/2	5/6/7	5/6/7	5/6/7	3/4
3	- education services	3	1	2	5/6/7	5/6/7	5/6/7	4
3	- hotel accommodation	x						
3	- living environment for highly qualified manpower	5	1/2	1/2	6/7	6/7	3/4	3/4
	Quality of accommodation							
5	- high-tech area	x						
5	- technically first-rate office	x						
4	- price level of territory	7	1	5/6	2/3/4	2/3/4	2/3/4	5/6
4	- price level of building	2	3	7	4/5/6	4/5/6	4/5/6	1

x An empty row means that all regions have been given the average score of 4: the criterion concerned has no distinctive quality.

Conclusion

The two information- and communication-intensive activities studied in this chapter, head offices and R & D, are both clearly concentrated in the core regions of the European Community. The explanation lies in the different locational endowment of core and other regions. The cost of telecommunication is a very important location factor, but some others, such as highly qualified manpower, are also major deterrminants of the locational choices made by R & D and HQ activities. Our analysis of the relative attractiveness of regions for the location of HQ and R & D has shown that the present concentration observed will not give way easily to deconcentration; indeed, the present relative positions are firmly attached to fundamental factors unlikely to change in the near future.

References

Ahnstrom (1973) *Styrande och ledande verksamhet i Vasteuropa, an ekonomisk geografisk studie*, Stockholm.

Armstrong, R. B. (1979) 'National trends in office construction, employment and headquarters location in US metropolitan areas', in P. W. Daniels (ed.) *Spatial Patterns of Office Growth and Location*, Chichester: Wiley.

Behrmann, J. N., and Fisher, W.A. (1980) *Overseas R&D Activities Transnational Companies*. Cambridge Mass.: Gelgeschlager, Gunn & Hain.

Beumer, L., Boeckhout, I. J., and Molle, W. (1984) *Factors Affecting Recent Changes in Urban Industrial and Office Location in the Netherlands*. Second International Congress of Arts and Sciences, Rotterdam

Boeckhout, I. J. *et al.* (1987) *Plaats en functie van de Randstad in de Nederlandse econimie* Rotterdam: NEI (mimeo).

Burns, L. S. (1977) 'The location of headquarters of industrial companies: a comment.' *Urban Studies* 14: 211-14.

Cameron, G. *et al.* (1981) *Highly Qualified Manpower and Unfavoured Regions*. Mimeo, Cambridge.

CEC (1987) *Third Periodic Report from the Commission on the Social and Economic Situation and Development of the Regions of the Community*. CEC: Brussels.

Coffey, W. J., and Polese, M. (1983) *Towards a Theory of the Inter-urban Location of Head Office Functions*, European Congress of Regional Science Association, Poitiers (mimeo).

Dunning, J. H. and Norman, G. (1979) *Factors Influencing the Loeation of Offices of Multinational Enterprises*. London: Location of Office Bureau (mimeo).
'The theory of multinational enterprises, an application to multinational office location.' *Environment and Planning* A. 15, 657-92.

Evans, A. W. (1973) 'The location of the headquarters of industrial companies.' *Urban Studies* 10: 387-96.

Firn, J. R. (1975) 'External control and regional development, the case of Scotland.' *Environment and Planning* 394-414.

Hart, H. W. ter (1980) *Vestigingsplaatsen van top management, verkenningen op het terrein van de transactionele geografie*, Amsterdam.

Howells, J.R.L. (1984) 'The location of research and development; some observations and evidence from Britain.' *Regional Studies*,18(1), 13-29.
IIM (1981) The mobilisation of the indigenous potential, Berlin, International Institute of Management.
Keizer, D. P. (1974) *De zelfstandigheid van de friese industrie in: te Keur voor Keuning*, Groningen.
Lloyd, P. E., and Dicken, P. (1977 *Location in Space*: London/New York.
Leyshon, A., Daniels, P. W., and Thrift, W. J. (1987) Large accountancy firms in the UK, operational adaptation and spatial development'. Working Paper on producer services, Liverpool.
McRae, H., and Cairncross, F. (1984) *Capital City: London as a Financial Centre*. London: Metheun.
Malecki, F. J. (1984) 'High technology and local economic development'. *Journal of the Amercian Planning Association*, 262-9.
Molle, W. T. M. (1983) 'Technological change and regional development in Europe.' Papers of the RSA, 52, 23-38. (1986) 'Regional impact of welfare state policies in the EC', in J.H.P. Paelinck (ed.), *Human Behaviour in Geographical Space*, Aldershot: Gower.
Molle, W. T. M., and Cappellin, R. (eds.), (1988) *Regional Impact of Community Policies in Europe*. Aldershot: Gower.
Molle, W. T. M., and Haselen, H. van (1987) *Divergence or Convergence between the Centre and the Periphery of Europe: An Analysis of Very Long Term Trends*. Rotterdam: NEI/FEER.
Molle, W. T. M., and Holst, B. van, (1984) 'Service et regions; une analyse des developpement a long terme services dan les regions de le CE.' *Revue d'Economie Regionale et Urbaine*, 5: 703-16.
Molle, W. T. M., with Holst, B. van, and Smit, H. (1980) *Regional Disparity and Economic Development in the EC*. Farnborough: Saxon House.
NBST (1987) STRIDE: *Science and Technology for Regional Innovation and Development in Europe*. Final Report. Dublin: NBST (mimeo).
RECLUS (1987) *Les Fonctions Internationales des Villes Europeennes*. Paris: Datar.
Smith, J. J. (1979) 'The effect of external take-overs on manufacturing employment change in the Northern Region 1963-1973.' *Regional Studies*, 421-39.
Thuis, M. J. T. and de Jong T. J. H. (1983) *Grote industriele ondernemingen in de Europese Gemeenschap* Utrech: GIRU, (mimeo).

15. Development of the information sector in the Basque Country

Juan Luis Llorens Urrutia

Basque Studies and Research Institute (IKEI)
San Sebastian, Spain

The purpose of this chapter is to highlight the importance that information development - in terms of content, accessibility and management - has for a society such as the Basque, which has reached a high degree of industrial and social development but is forced, in order to maintain it, to assimilate new technologies which ultimately involve a change in work organisation, production management and even leisure.

The implementation of new information technologies in traditional sectors of the Basque economy is bringing about a production system which can flexibly respond to information signals. The changes being brought about by information or computerisation open up the possibility of integrating the production system into the total external and internal information system of the firm. The relevance of information technology therefore lies not so much in access to information as in the translation of information into the productive and organisational processes of the firm.

One must not think that these mutations are new barriers to the development of small and medium enterprises, or that they are limited to firms of a certain size. On the contrary, new information technologies are particularly appropriate for small and medium enterprises and, in fact, allow for an even greater degree of decentralisation - both geographical and internal. To a certain extent, instant information transmission shatters the strategic importance of physical space.

The development of the information sector is a complex process. It involves public-sector actions in development of the infrastructure, in stimulating awareness and in training as well as parallel change in the structure and capacity of firms. The Autonomous Administration of the Basque Country has undertaken a number of programmes to boost adoption and use of information technology, and surveys show that the industrial sector has begun to modernise. Industrialists know that it is a matter of survival and essential in maintaining a competitive edge in an open European market.

Importance of information technology for business

The role and evolution of information in business

1. Planning
2. Execution
3. Result evaluation

The need for evaluation originated the first information system. However, evaluation is not an end in itself: one needs to know in order to act, or if results are negative, to react. Thus, an evaluation system is efficient inasmuch as it conveys information quickly and accurately, and allows for fast and appropriate reactions. In a competitive context, information processing is a strategic factor for a firm's success.

Computer information systems reduce analysis - and therefore reaction times within the firm. This fact has direct implications not only on evaluation but also on production. For instance, making financial transactions easier reduces costs, but computerising client orders allows for better production co-ordination, thus reducing the need to keep finished products, intermediate or raw materials in stock, and resulting in more significant savings.

In addition, computerising design production activities (CAD/CAM) not only shortens production times but also permits more flexible and diversified product series at competitive costs. In fact, it shifts the advantages of scale to small enterprises. Further, computerising these processes permits physical decentralisation and disaggregation of production units without losing the advantages of proximity, in so far as the transmission of information through local networks and electronic mail services takes place simultaneously.

Bringing computers and microelectronics into production permits the creation of new products, not only capital goods (numerically controlled machinery, etc.) but also consumer goods (cameras, hi-fi systems, applicances, automobiles, etc.) and services (automatic flight reservation and certain financial products, etc.).

Finally, the firm's planning activities are also affected. Strategic decision-making must take both internal and external information into account. Information (or doubts) regarding changes in the environment, such as competitiors' activities, technological innovations, new markets, regulatory developments, and so on, affect planning directly, whether the firm is actively or passively involved.

The development of information processing fosters the growth of a series of service firms (both private and public) which gather, produce and make information available to potential users through some kind of database (reference databases, bibliographies, directories, source databases numbers, texts, text-numbers, images ... mixed databases). Access to databases, which generally takes place through distributing firms, is thus a strategically important factor.

The firm's capacity to adjust to information technology innovations

The firm's relation to the new information technologies is global. It covers all its activities: management (internal information), production (control and design) and planning (knowledge of the environment and decision-making regarding production, sales and investment based on internal and external information). It is not a matter of automatising this or that application but of redesigning the firm's activity and organising it based on the new technologies - their modes of production, access to markets, relations with clients and suppliers, the definition of their products, and so on.

For small and medium enterprises, which constitute the majority in both the Basque and Spanish economies, it is highly unlikely that a radical change in the firms' organisation can take place overnight, as if it were a matter of buying a new car or a new machine. The process is in fact quite complex: it implies changes in specific production processes, changes in accounting and management organisation, changes in organisational structure, in short, changes in human resources, personnel training and behaviour. Some of these changes can be made 'from outside,' that is through technical consultants external to the firm. Even the whole organisation of the firm may be redefined by a systems and organisation consulting firm. But the implementation of new systems requires that personnel be adequately trained to operate them. The educational process - at all levels within the firm - is most important.

It is important that the firm's personnel and management have the computer skills to allow them to take advantage of the potential offered by new technologies. Factors such as the firm's computer history, the level and experience of its technicians and, especially, the degree of integration of computing into the firm's activities, are important as are the computerisation of the various management functions, as well as production; the use of programming in production through various automated means (from numerical control to robotics); personnel experience with PCs, terminals, programming, databases, and so on, and finally, the integration of computer planning and control into the firm's strategic and planning activities.

It is always possible to skip stages, especially for new firms, but a reasonable computer implementation process - considering this not as a goal in itself, but a means through which the 'information technology revolution' is assimilated into the firm - may comprise the following stages:

1. Computerisation of basic management functions (general accounting, billing, payroll, etc.). Intensification of the process.
2. Computerisation of basic production functions (warehouse control, sales, management, post-sales service, design, quality control, etc.) Integration of management and production control functions.
3. Isolated introduction of automated elements into the production chain (numerical control or other programmable automated elements). Integration of design and manufacturing functions. Interconnection of programmable automated elements.
4. Computerised connection of programmable auomated elements (building of a local industrial network). Connection of 'production computer' with central computer (building of a local production management network).

Parallel to this internal computerisation process, the firm may join external telematic networks for obtaining external information, for example from technological or socioeconomic databases, for making various kinds of transactions (banking, sales, etc.) or for interconnecting various physically dispersed firm units. These functions are certainly independent from the above - mentioned stages, but it is clear that the propensity to use them will depend on the degree of familarisation with computer techniques.

In the Basque Country, where there is a long-standing tradition of mechanised industries to which the advantages of automation are clear, the starting-point is quite favourable. In addition, the awareness of the need for technological renewal in order to overcome the crisis has created a fertile background for innovation. And even though interest in innovation has focused more on manufacturing technology than on management, sales or organisation, computer innovations spread very easily. Familiarisation with techniques and instruments has an educational effect which goes beyond those immediately involved, fostering their introduction to other areas of the firm. As we shall see, the public and semi-public sector have played a major role in this familiarisation process.

The role of the public sector

The agents of change

The Autonomous Basque Administration has played a key role as promoter of industrial renewal in the Basque Country, especially through the Society for Industrial Promotion and Retransformation (SPRI), a public company affiliated with the Basque government's Department of Industry and Energy. Other active participants in the process, not always in a co-ordinated fashion, have been the regional governments of Guipuzcoa and Vizcaya, the former through various sponsorship programmes (industrial investment, technology centres, database consulting) and the latter through the more aggressive programmes of its Economic Promotion and Development Department, such as the creation of R & D groups specialising in automation and robotics, a business information centre, and so on. At the same time, private enterprise created a public teledocumentation unit in 1979, at the Institute of Basque Studies and Research (IKEI), which was afterwards extended to other centres.

Support programmes in the public sector: SPRI

Looking back, one may see how SPRI has fostered gradual implementation of computer applications in Basque industry, through specific, temporary and targeted programmes, so that six years after its inception, after having reached enough people in industry, it was able to launch an ambitious programme geared to telematic development as recently as 23 May 1988.

Typical programmes undertaken by SPRI are:

1. CN-100, launched in 1983 with the manifest intention of promoting the purchase and thus manufacture of 100 numerical control machines through subsidies. The programme was based on the existence of an important machine - tool manufacturing sector which was in crisis and in need of technological renewal. The incorporation of microelectronics was their only salvation.
2. ECTA programme promoted the purchase and development of technologically advanced equipment, and was unrestricted as to type of equipment or sector of industry.
3. IMI programme, literally incorporation of microelectronics in industry, commenced at the end of 1984. It focused on processes rather than equipment, subsidising feasibility studies and implementation. In so doing, it fostered service companies and technological supply to industry. The programme also performs training in computing and microelectronic techniques in order to remedy the shortage of qualified personnel. A bulletin, *IMI News*, has 60,000 subscribers and 4,000 people have attended courses.
4. The Spritel programme created the first public telematic network in

Spain. It links the three capitals of the Autonomous Community and can be accessed by anyone with a compatible terminal. Its software allows access to the various systems in use throughout the world. It is hoped that in conjunction with other economic incentives a varied supply of telematics services will develop.

Other programmes which are stimulating the expansion of computerisation in Basque industry include the soft-loan programme for investments in technology; the enchancement of five privately - run technology centres by financing the purchase of new equipment, hiring of research personnel and subsidising joint research projects; subsidies for R&D units in industrial firms.

Together all of these contributed to the formation of an adequate breeding ground for technological awareness, whose lack was so deeply felt at the beginning of the crisis.

The regional governments

Basque regional governments have also contributed part of their budgets to the promotion of industrial innovation and development, mainly through investment subsidies or through support given to technology centres in their areas. Innovation projects receive higher subsidy rates from incentive programmes. In the case of the Vizcaya government, two research groups related to automation and robotics have been created.Moreover, the regional governments support those activities specifically related to infomtion which are not included in the Autonomous Administration's programmes. For instance, the government of Guipozcoa subsidises up to 25 per cent of the cost of telematic enquiries through the two companies who offer this public service. The government of Vizcaya has created its own public teledocumentation centre within its Centre for Business Information, where Basque companies can have their questions answered for free. Apart from the fact that their pricing policy is more than debatable, there is no doubt that both have the effect of promoting the access of companies to the world of referential or factual databases. We will later comment on the results obtained so far in this area.

Spread of computing, automation and telematics among Basque industries

Introduction

Given the importance of technological innovation, it is always tempting to enquire about the degree of penetration of specific techniques. This is not easy, since what really matters is to determine the effects of such penetration in terms of social and economic results. Hence, even though the above-mentioned government promotional activities may seem impressive, we must not forget we are dealing with a change of mentality and attitudes and not just with the introduction of a machine or technique. In short, it is to be expected that effective introduction will be costly. Despite this, several recent surveys have tackled this question, and shown, taking into account the shortcomings of the surveying techniques, the relative degree of penetration. In the following sections, a sample of the results obtained is given.

Penetration of computing in Basque industry

IKEI surveys give a preliminary evaluation of the degree of penetration of computing in Basque industrial companies. At the beginning of 1984, 42 per cent had computerised at least one management function but only 20 per cent were considering expanding or introducing functions. Four years later, these percentages grew to 73 per cent and 50 per cent, respectively, as seen in Table 15.1. At the same time, computer use has become more intensive, moving from three to five computerised functions.

Table 15.1 Computerisation of management functions, by firm size

	% Computerised		No. of functions	
Employees	1984	1988	1984	1988
1-49	34.7	41.0	2.9	3.9
50-99	69.4	96.8	3.2	4.7
100-249	73.5	95.7	3.9	5.6
250-499	94.0	94.4	4.5	5.7
+500	96.7	100.0	5.3	6.5
TOTAL	41.5	73.1	3.2	5.1

Even though management functions are still those which are more frequently computerised (among these, general accounting, 96 per cent billing, 84 per cent and payroll, 78 per cent), there is a strong movement towards computerisation of production functions (Table 15.2). Before, only 6 per cent had computerised at least one production function; the percentage is now 47 per cent (warehouse management, 79 per cent production planning, 68 per cent. On the other hand, design is one of the least computerised functions, with 21 per cent). The intensity of computerisation is also lower, but continues to grow: from 2.4 functions four years ago, to 3.8 today. In Tables 15.1 and 15.2 we may see the relationship between firm size and degree of computerisation: firms with less than 100 employees show computerisation levels below the mean.

Table 15.2 Computerisation of production functions, by firm size

Employees	% Computerised 1984	% Computerised 1988	No. of functions 1984	No. of functions 1988
1-49	2.7	23.0	2.7	2.9
50-99	18.1	64.5	2.3	3.5
100-249	17.6	52.2	2.0	4.2
250-499	44.0	66.7	2.8	4.1
+500	60.0	83.3	2.9	4.1
TOTAL	6.2	46.9	2.4	3.8

Productive process automation

The introduction of programmable automated elements has also experienced a strong boost, as expected after the orientation given to industry policy: while in 1984, 13 per cent of firms had some component of this kind, in 1988 the percentage has increased dramatically, to 20 per cent.

Table 15. 3 Computerised management functions (% of computerised firms)

	1984	1988
General accounting	93.3	95.5
Payroll	70.1	77.1
Invoicing	64.6	83.9
Inventory management	39.3	68.8
Analytical accounting	19.5	41.5
Purchases	14.7	51.8
Financial management	n/a	39.3
After-sales service	7.2	15.6
Others	7.0	8.9

Table 15. 4 Computerised production functions (% of computerised firms)

	1984	1988
Warehouse management	64.5	79.4
Production planning	50.0	67.6
Work - in - progress scheduling	41.9	42.6
Labour scheduling	32.3	47.1
Machinery scheduling	24.2	36.8
Budgets	17.7	38.2
Quality control	14.5	29.4
Design	3.2	20.6
Others	1.6	1.5

However, there is much to be done to achieve a new productive organisation, since the programmable elements are mostly isolated: only 5 per cent of firms have a local industrial network (20 per cent of the programmable automated elements are connected to a computer) and only 2 per cent a local management network.

In 8 per cent of firms some type of industrial robot has been installed, usually of the 'pick and place' kind, and in 33 per cent of the cases, these robots perform more complex functions. Nevertheless, a significant improvement has been made in relation to four years ago, when only 0.5 per cent of surveyed firms had robots. Moreover, 11 per cent are considering introducing robots, since they are familiar with their applications in industry (31 per cent of those surveyed) (Table 15.5).

Table 15.5 Automation and robots in Basque industry (% of all firms)

	1984	1988
With programmable automated elements	12.9	20.3
• Interconnected		4.0
• Local industrial network		4.7
• Local management network		1.3
Robot	0.5	8.0
• 'Pick and place'		6.0
• Other functions		2.7
Consider introducing robots		10.7

Introduction of telematics

Telematics, defined as the possibility of accessing or transmitting computer information through telecommunication systems, is, in general, fairly well known (49 per cent of surveyed firms) among firms in the Basque Country, where access to reference databases began ten years ago.

However, only 8 per cent of the firms have used this system at least once. As usual, the expectation to use this system in the future is greater: 26 per cent think it is likely, but admit not having prepared personnel (except 12 per cent of the cases). Before the Spritel network was inaugurated, 27 per cent of the firms knew about the project, even-though the majority knew nothing about the existence of institutional aids in this respect (78 per cent) and others considered the latter insufficient (12 per cent).

Aside from the results of the survey - which, because of the low number of users does not allow too much detail - the long history of teledocumentation centres gives us another way of examining the penetration of these services in the industrial sector.

The Business Development Centre, whose area of activity comprises all of the Basque Country, but in fact operates mostly in Guipuzcoa, handled 707 reference questions in 1987, 60 per cent from Guipuzcoa, 29 per cent from Vizcaya and 7 per cent from Alava. Expansion has been rapid, growing from eighty reference questions recorded by IKEI in 1979, but has slowed down in the past year. To these figures we should add another 200 reference questions made to databases managed by the Business Information Centre of the government of Vizcaya (Table 15.6).

Table 15. 6 Enquiries to databases

	Enquiries	Documents
1984	172	501
1985	407	828
1986	650	1,827
1987	707	2,021

Source : Business Development Centre

None the less, only 50 per cent of the total number of enquiries may be attributed directly to firms, while the rest originated in the sponsorsed technology centres. This peculiarity (together with the proximity of the Business Development Centre) accounts for the greater use of databases in Guipuzcoa, since four out of five of these centres are located in its territory.

Conclusions

In view of the advances made in the techniques related to information management, we must conclude that the gradual but ever-widening development policy followed in the Basque Country, has been appropriate. The severity of the crisis and the consequent conviction that technological development was the way out, have contributed to the policy's success. The Basque Country's productive structure, relying heavily on industrial component and equipment manufacturing, was particularly appropriate for an industrial computerisation process. However, the development of the telematic service industry encounters greater difficulties. The implementation of Spritel will definitely contribute to the extension of these services to the public, who make up a sizable market related to consumption and leisure. This development is undoubtedly a challenge, but the outlook is favourable.

Index